No Longer Last on the List

A self-growth guide for tired, busy women; helping you to eliminate doubt, set boundaries and prioritise you own importance, without guilt.

By Jo Bevilacqua

Self Published by Jo Bevilacqua
Printed by Book Printing UK www.bookprintinguk.com
Remus House, Coltsfoot Drive, Peterborough, PE2 9BF
Printed in Great Britain

ISBN: 978-1-5272-7452-5

Contents

Foreword

Have you ever felt like life is a never-ending to-do list where everyone else's needs come before your own?

Partner, mother, daughter, friend, niece, aunt, employee, boss, carer. Women are required to fill so many roles and yet face societal pressures and expectations about every choice they make.

The truth is you can never make everyone happy, at least not all the time! There will always be people who judge you unfairly or disagree with your choices. The only way forward is to rise above other people's opinions and start putting yourself at the top of your priority list.

This book breaks down the barriers that hold you back and offers you practical activities to both inspire and motivate you. It encourages you to seek out more of what lights you up inside and to recognise and do something about the parts of your life that don't serve you anymore.

Jo Bevilacqua is an award-winning entrepreneur with three successful businesses, and a mum of two. She shows up every day for a large community of women to help them launch and run their own businesses but truthfully, she is a cheerleader to all women. She understands from first-hand experience the pressures on women that still exist today and helps you to thrive, not just survive.

Throughout the book she's by your side as a friend and mentor, urging you on and inviting you to celebrate everything that makes you a person worth prioritising.

It's time to put yourself FIRST on the list … and that starts with this book!

Go read it!

Shaa Wasmund MBE, Sunday Times best-selling author

Introduction

Do you feel like something in your life needs to change? Is it time you started putting yourself at the top of your never-ending to-do list?

The fact that you've picked up this book and you're reading it right now means you're ready to start prioritising your own needs, once and for all.

This book has been written to give you – the woman who is everything to everyone around you – the permission and tools to put yourself first for what I can imagine will be the first time in a very long while.

So, if you're fed up and exhausted from …

* firefighting all day, every day

* juggling what feels like a million different plates

* never having a minute to yourself because you're trying to keep everyone else happy, even at your own detriment

* fixing everyone else's problems, even when you've enough of your own stuff to sort

* knowing you need to make changes but not having the confidence to do so

* wondering how everyone else seems to have their sh*t together, while you feel that your life is passing you by in a flash

… it's time to make a change, starting today. Let's do it together.

What you need to know about this book

Firstly, this is not a 'self-help' book. I would describe it more as a 'self-growth' book.

Secondly, this is NOT a 'once-and-done' book either (you know, the book that you read once and put on the shelf to collect dust). It's a book that has been written in the hope that you will use it over and over again, no matter where you are in your life.

Thirdly, I imagine some of the chapters will speak to you, while others might not. That's OK. Take what you need from this book and park the rest, but read it all, even if you don't think it's relevant at the time. As you read through, you might get some insight into how some of your girlfriends or female relations are feeling, even if something doesn't resonate with you. Maybe the book will be a conversation starter.

Finally, this is NOT a book that has been written by a person claiming to be an 'expert in life' or to have all the answers. It is written by a 36-year-old woman who knows from experience how hard it was to put herself on the list at all, let alone at the top of it.

Whether you read the whole book in one sitting or it takes you weeks, the only thing I ask is that you commit to reading it from start to finish. You could say it's the first and most important activity of the book, to start and finish something for yourself!

Speaking of activities, you'll find them throughout this book. They're all activities that I use in real-life and have fine-tuned over the years. If you don't want to write in the book, you can print off free copies of the activity sheets online at: https://www.jobevilacqua.com/resources/

I have a feeling that this is going to be amazing for you and I'm so glad that I can share this journey with you. Lots of love, Jo x

When a flower
doesn't bloom, you
fix the environment
in which it grows,
not the flower

-Alexander Den Heijer

Chapter 1:

Are you always bottom of the list?

(It's time to stop comparing yourself to others' highlight reels and take a priority place on your own to-do list)

Hey, how are you?

Fine? OK? Great?

I mean, HONESTLY... How are YOU?

Tired, busy, frazzled, or lost, even?

Too tired to read this properly, so pretty thankful it's formatted to be easy to scan?

I'm guessing you're not only physically tired but you're probably mentally tired too.

Tired from the multiple plates you're constantly spinning. Tired from the neverending list of things to do. Tired from the responsibilities and expectations thrown upon you from what sometimes feels like every single human being in your life.

I get it, I really do. You have somehow just 'got' to this point and you can't see how things can change. It's almost like Groundhog Day.

But I am telling you it needs to stop.

It really needs to stop now.

You need to stop putting yourself last.

You need to stop agreeing to do things when you don't want to do them. Stop saying 'yes' when what you really want to say is 'no'. Stop going out if you want to stay at home (or staying at home if you want to go out). Stop feeling like you have to do more or be more to matter.

Stop killing yourself slowly to make sure everyone around you is happy even though by doing so is to your own detriment.

Enough is enough.

Something needs to change and that change is going to start today.

Imagine feeling energetic and excited to get up every morning. Imagine only spending time with people who make you feel good - good about yourself and good about the world. Imagine only going to places that you genuinely want to go to, that you know are going to make you smile and lift you up inside.

How much happier would you feel?

How much more energy would you have?

How much more would you love yourself, the people around you and the life you lead?

What are you waiting for? Let's get to it.

Activity One: Discovering what really matters

I've got a quick activity for you to get things started.

I want you to sit down for ten minutes somewhere you won't be distracted.

 This might be at home on your sofa when everyone else is out, in the car while waiting to pick your kids up or while you're on the toilet pretending to go for a number two because that's the only time you can get more than two minutes to yourself (although if your kids are like mine, even that is a struggle. Anyone else's kids NEED a cuddle while you're on the loo?!).

Wherever you are, I'd like you to use these ten minutes to write a list of all of the important things in your life. Start with number one being the most important thing and work your way down, thinking of all the things you do day-to-day, week-to-week, month-to-month.

Note: You will find a template on the next page or you can print off a copy from the my website at: https://www.jobevilacqua.com/resources/

The list of priorities could include people, responsibilities, hobbies, commitments or even words that resonate with you.

Put a timer on your phone and try and stay focused until it goes off. Try not to overthink – just jot down whoever or whatever comes to mind.

PRIORITY ORDER

Write a list of all the important things in your life.

1._____

2._____

3._____

4._____

5._____

6._____

7._____

8._____

9._____

10._____

Now you've done this exercise, what does the list tell you? Any revelations? Was there confirmation of what you knew already?

More importantly, how do you feel? Stressed, overwhelmed, validated?

When I do this with women in both group sessions and one-to-one, it's always an activity that creates a lot of emotion. It isn't until the women take a few minutes to write down in black and white everything they do, that they allow themselves permission to stop and digest.

When asked, many of the women have – without hesitation – told me with pride and conviction that the number one priority on their list is their children and that pretty much everything they do, they do for them. Although I understand that when you have children you would walk through fire for them (as I would for my own children), it's important to recognise that you can't pour from an empty cup.

You can't give 100% if you don't feel 100%.

What also transpires from this activity is that most women don't put themselves in the top ten of their lists. The top ten is usually filled with people, work and chores around the house.

In fact, at my December 2019 networking event, 17 out of the 24 attendees put themselves either last on the list or not on the list at all. Out of the whole group, only two put themselves at the top and both of those women openly shared they were only aware that they needed to do so after suffering from mental or physical health issues in the past.

17 out of 24 – I mean, what the hell?!

While I agree that we can't just sack off everything in our lives – for example, our work, partners, friends or house – to do what we want, surely we have to agree that we NEED to be more of a priority on our own lists?

We certainly need to be on there at the very least, right?

Who you are now and where you are in life

To make any sort of change you need to first establish and accept where you are right now, mentally as well as physically. There may be parts of your life that you absolutely love. That's fantastic. I want you to celebrate those things and then use this book to figure out how you can have more of them. And if there's stuff that doesn't feel quite as good, we're going to work on how you can change things for the better or even let go of what doesn't serve you anymore.

First things first – you can't make changes without knowing WHAT you need to change and hopefully this book will help you figure that out.

But it will be a process. Like using sat nav to get you from one place to another. Not only do you need to know where you're going but also where you are now: your current location. If you don't have either of these bits of information, good luck trying to find your way!

I've learnt that there is an overwhelming number of people who struggle to accept where they are now, who are living in the past or craving SOMETHING for their future; they're just not sure what. There is also a huge number of people who don't know where they want to go, who they want to be or what actually makes them happy.

Now, this could be down to a number of reasons: low confidence, fear, procrastination, the inability to dream big, a lack of self-awareness or good old complacency are just a few. And just so you know, whatever the reason there's absolutely no judgement at all from me.

It's OK if you fit into one or many of those categories right now. Hopefully, I'm going to shake things up a bit and get you moving – your very own Joe Wicks of getting your life in shape!

I think it's important to acknowledge that the person you are now is not only the result of things you have experienced recently but an accumulation of all the things that have happened to you during your lifetime.

All of the experiences you have gone through, good and bad, all of the judgements and opinions of others that you have come across and held on to, the expectations heaped upon you by other people, starting from when you were a child.

You may have been brought up to believe, or have come to the conclusion yourself, that to be a good person you have to do everything for everyone and that everyone else's needs are somehow your responsibility. You might even believe that it's down to you to keep everything together and everyone around you happy, even when it means you continuously put yourself last.

Regardless of whether you have put this great amount of pressure on yourself or it has been put upon you by other people, if it's not making you happy, you can change it, if that's what you want to do.

Something's got to change

So, I'm assuming that if you've got this far, you probably agree that something in your life needs to change. Or maybe it's not one thing but multiple things!

Believe me when I tell you, you're not the first to feel this and I guarantee you won't be the last.

Maybe you feel like you could do with tweaking a few things to feel calmer and more fulfilled. Perhaps you're drowning in responsibility. Maybe you feel overwhelmed from the minute you open your eyes to the minute you close them at night or maybe you just never have a minute to catch a breath, let alone a break.

Perhaps it cuts a little bit deeper though. Maybe you look at your life and think, how did I get here? How is this my reality? Why do I not feel happy or content?

You could be that person who everyone else thinks has it all together – an inspiration even? On paper you agree, everything does look perfect, but deep down you know something just doesn't feel right. You just may not know what that something is yet and that's ok. You're not supposed to know all the answers.

Did you miss the class on 'how to thrive as an adult' too?

Over the last few years, I have worked with many women. What's become apparent is that most of them believe that everyone else has their sh*t together, while they're clearly the only one to have missed the class at school on 'how to be a functioning adult' because they're just surviving day by day. It doesn't help either that everyone is so keen to share their highlight reel on social media and in person.

You know what it's like when you bump into people at the supermarket or the school gates and they can't wait to tell you about all the great stuff going on in their lives – the new house, new car, the job promotions, the engagements, their amazing kids achieving amazing stuff, and the fact that their dog can actually wipe its own backside. OK, so that last bit about the dog is probably an exaggeration but sometimes it does actually feel like that, right?

And let's not forget the parents at the school gates who know EVERYTHING about everything. The ones that always home-make mountains of stuff for the bake sale, that never need reminding about the open afternoons and who always rustle up the perfect World Book Day costume. While you, on the other hand, sometimes feel like you've climbed Mount Everest just getting your kids to school on time, clean and fed, without losing your fricking mind.

Then there's social media, which just amplifies the belief that everyone but you is in on the secret of living 'successfully', whatever this means to you. When all we see on people's profiles are the exciting things going on in their lives, it's hard to remember that these same people will have their own struggles and insecurities too, they're just not sharing them with the world, just like you.

Although other people's lives are of great interest to most of us, and that's human nature, they're also one of the greatest distractions that stop us from creating our own happiness. When we fill our time with watching reality TV programmes, scrolling the news feed and obsessing over celebs, we don't allow the time to value or change our own life, or if we do, we only do so to compare, not to grow.

Accepting change

Even if we're able to put the 'comparisonitis' to one side, one thing I have noticed with women is that we struggle to accept change within OURSELVES.

It's hard to accept the fact that every significant situation in our lives can change us internally, change the person we are, change our expectations, our confidence and our boundaries.

Many of us pine for the person we once were – the young, innocent, care-free soul that found fun in everything we did. We yearn to be the person who was open and trusting, who embraced anything, everything and everyone. The person who had never been hurt and who had few responsibilities.

Or, on the flip side, some of us would do anything not to remember or be the person we once were and all that we have done to escape the past. Sometimes, this refusal to reflect back on our journey can be as limiting as always looking backwards and longing for time gone by.

So, how do we go about accepting the change within ourselves? How do we learn to feel at peace with who we are without measuring it against anyone else or another time in our life?

That's what we're going to tackle together in this book. It may not be easy at times, but it will be so worthwhile.

Reflection time

Before you move on to the next chapter, it would be great if you could take a few minutes to reflect on what we've just covered. You can make some notes here or you can download your free Reflection Journal from https://www.jobevilacqua.com/resources/

You will see these 'reflection time' pages throughout the book. It is a great tool for you to use and a reminder to take some time to process each chapter, acknowledge what you have learnt and what you need to change, if anything.

REFLECTION TIME

How do you feel?

_____

_____

_____

What have you learnt?

_____

_____

_____

What will you change?

_____

_____

_____

What will you do more of?

_____

_____

_____

What will you do less of?

_____

_____

_____

Does this raise any strong feelings for you?
(This is your gut telling you that there's a potential issue you need to address)

_____

_____

_____

Do you have any questions?

_____

_____

_____

Chapter 2:

My story

(From party girl with no direction to
Stepford wife to happy entrepreneur)

Writing this book wasn't half as easy as I thought it would be. Even though I put the outline of the book and the chapters together in about an hour while brainstorming with a friend, actually writing it was a million times harder.

I knew the message I wanted to convey from day one but I was so worried about offending people, writing the wrong thing, or that people might think I was judging them and their decisions, that I experienced writer's block more times than I wish to admit.

I had to fight against the feeling of hypocrisy as, to be honest with you, I too am the woman who has struggled to put herself on the list, let alone at the top of it! I too have been the woman that puts everything and everyone over my own wants and needs.

I'd often ask myself, who am I to tell you what I believe you should be doing when sometimes I struggle to do it myself?

In other words, I had a major attack of the dreaded 'Imposter Syndrome'.

But, as I tell other people almost daily, you don't have to be perfect at something to believe in it or to be able to share it with others. It's OK to just be part of the conversation.

That was one of two things that kept me going and why you're holding this book reading it right now. That and when I told people what I wanted to write about they told me I HAD to do it, for them, their sister, their best friend and every other woman they know!

Which, of course, was equally as lovely as it was petrifying!

So, the fact is that I'm not perfect and I don't follow my own advice 100% of the time. Still, more often than not these days, I DO ensure that I'm at the top of my own list because I truly believe I HAVE to be. Just because I'm not at the top of the list 100% of the time doesn't make me a hypocrite. It makes me human, genuine, relatable, real, and that's all I want to be.

I have experienced great things in my life but there have also been times when life has been pretty naff too. I've grown and changed so much that there were moments when I found it hard to recognise myself in the mirror. Sometimes I felt lost even when everyone else thought I had it all.

In all honesty, that perception is probably what almost stopped me writing this more than anything else in the world.

Although I adore my family, friends and my work, I sometimes find myself looking back on the past and craving to be the person I was before, even for a few hours. You know, the younger, slimmer, funnier, stress and responsibility-free version of me.

Fortunately, these moments are fleeting these days, or maybe it's just that I allow these thoughts to come without beating myself up about feeling them. Either way, I'm happy enough with who I am today to accept all the changes I've been through since those care-free days.

How did I get here?

The potted history of my adult life is quite the rollercoaster.

I entered my late teens as a bit of a party girl and that pretty much followed me into adulthood. I was that girl who was ALWAYS in a bar or club with at least one alcopop in my hand, if not a tray of shots!

In many ways, I was the definition of a functional borderline alcoholic, sugar-coated as a party animal. A young girl working hard and partying harder was pretty much the norm in the early 2000s; if you hit adulthood in that era, you probably know what I mean!

I had a few relationships in those years, most were healthy but a couple not so much. Those bad relationships played havoc with my self-esteem and confidence and I had no real direction in my life.

But then I met my husband and what started out as a bit of fun ended up with him moving in with me four months later and getting pregnant a month after that. You could say that it quickly went from no strings attached to being strung together for the rest of our lives – after all, there's no bigger bond than having kids together.

I was determined that life would be 'perfect' and that I would be the best partner/wife and mum that I could be. I look back on those as my Stepford wife years!

During my pregnancy with my oldest daughter, I worked in a nursery and saw so many parents who wanted to attend things we were doing but weren't able to due to work. That observation, coupled with my employers trying to demote me when I fell pregnant and my partner having problems getting extended parental leave, changed my future.

I swore that no-one would dictate to us what we could or couldn't experience as parents. Attending assemblies, Christmas plays, sports days and all of those other childhood milestones were non-negotiable for me. I was completely obsessed with being there for my daughter at all costs.

It was during this period of maternity leave in August 2009 that my husband and I set up a business together: Hallmark Carpets and Flooring. It was my first experience of running a business and self-employment.

I completely loved being a mum, but I also realised that it wasn't up to my daughter or husband to give me a purpose in life or to define my worth. That was too much pressure and responsibility to put on them, so I had to find my worth in my own right too.

A month after launching our business, I started a degree in Childhood Studies as I wanted to prove to myself that the girl who dropped out of sixth form, and then college a year later, could get a degree.

As I neared the end of the course, and while I was pregnant with our second daughter, a random conversation resulted in me being unable to stop thinking about how amazing it would be to create a hair salon with an on-site crèche, a safe haven that gave stressed-out mums a break.

Within four weeks I had a 40-page business plan and started looking for premises. I was eight months pregnant. It never got boring watching the commercial property agents' faces gape in shock as a heavily pregnant lady got out the car to look around empty units, some near derelict.

Many people thought my obsession with opening the salon would diminish when I had the baby but the opposite happened. My salon, Serenity Loves, opened in 2012. Word of mouth about the salon exploded on social media and, throughout 2013 and 2014, we received numerous business accolades, recognition and awards, both locally and nationally.

By 2016, I was able to step out of the day-to-day running of the salon, knowing that it was in the hands of an amazing team that I had trained and knew I could trust.

Being semi-retired at 32 sounds amazing, right? But as great as it sounds on paper, I struggled to adapt to my new reality. My days were left empty as the girls were at school and everyone else was at work.

Thinking about all I had learned from running two businesses, I launched The Unique Mumpreneur to help women set up and/or grow their own businesses while raising their families.

I've recently rebranded that business under my own name Jo Bevilacqua and I have a much bigger vision for what I want to achieve. Not only do I want to help all business owners to grow their businesses, I want to create a space where women can come together and support each other personally as well as professionally, hence writing this book.

These days, I am very grateful for my life. I'm a wife, mum, daughter, sister, aunt, business owner, friend and creator but, above all, I'm Jo.

What my experiences have taught me

What I've learned from life so far is that we're never just meant to be one person. We are constantly evolving and our priorities shift. But, for some reason, we are conditioned to never be our own priority.

It's normal to put everything and everyone else first and, although evolving is human nature, if we evolve towards our own wants and needs it's often frowned upon by the people around us.

Something else I've observed is that, more often than not, women are defined by their relationships with their children (more about this in the next chapter!). Although we're in 2020, women are still made to feel bad for wanting to work, pursue a hobby or other passion while raising their children, in a way that men aren't.

Have you experienced that?

I felt it myself when I became a mum.

While my husband was praised for making the leap from employment to self-employment, many questioned whether I was making the right decision. People asked about mine and the children's emotions and bonds but never thought to ask the same of my husband. I was asked how I would juggle it all. Was I worried it would affect the children? Not one person asked my husband this.

I will always remember one person asking me, 'why don't you just want to be a good mum?' as if being a working mum would affect my parenting and my children's development in a way that was somehow different to my working husband.

The truth is that as much as I love my children, and believe me, I would go to the end of the earth for them, I've always wanted to achieve something for myself. I don't believe that my wants and needs should be diminished or brushed aside because I'm a mum. No woman should.

I had to give myself permission to feel that and not to be affected by other people's opinions or I would have driven myself crazy, forced into a box or a role that I didn't want and would never be happy with.

I'm glad that I decided to stand up for myself and my potential and didn't succumb to other people's expectations. It definitely wasn't easy, but it was so worthwhile.

Above all, I've learned that I have to live in a way that feels authentic to me and to my precious family. I know that I will continue to grow and evolve and that's alright because that's what life is all about – a journey, a process, progress. I hope this book gives you the permission to stand up for yourself and your potential, to stop giving to other people's expectations and to live your life in a way that feels authentic to you. Otherwise, you're just standing still, and you and I were not born to stand still.

REFLECTION TIME

How do you feel?

_____

_____

_____

What have you learnt?

_____

_____

_____

What will you change?

_____

_____

_____

What will you do more of?

_____

_____

_____

What will you do less of?

_____

_____

_____

Does this raise any strong feelings for you?
(This is your gut telling you that there's a potential issue you need to address)

_____

_____

_____

Do you have any questions?

_____

_____

_____

Chapter 3:

Mum's the word

(Why it's OK to want more than motherhood)

Before we dive deeper into the book and start working on some of the game-changing activities that I use with my mentoring clients, I want to talk a bit more about motherhood.

Although I don't exclusively mentor working mums and this book certainly isn't for mums only, I do find that most of the women in my network are wrestling with motherhood in some way, even if it's in the context of if or when it might fit into their lives - or not.

I want to take a moment to acknowledge this and touch on how this might affect how you prioritise yourself.

"Where was the mother?"

Years ago, I was watching a random programme about a serial killer (as you do!) and the narrator talked about the killer's mother. The tone almost implied that she had allowed her son to become a monster and that she was responsible for his crimes.

When I was young, I remember hearing about a child getting hurt in an accident and people saying, 'Where was his mother? Wasn't she watching him?'

On both of those occasions it struck me that when something goes awry in a young person's life, people rarely ask, 'Where was the father?' in the same accusatory tone. And yet all eyes turn to the mother.

It's as though women are meant to exist in permanent orbit around their offspring.

I remember realising quite early in life that women are often defined in relation to their role as a mother, or the absence of that role.

Think about famous child-free women such as Jennifer Anniston, Kylie Minogue or Kim Cattrall. They almost constantly have to defend their decision not to have had children to the press and their so-called 'adoring' public.

Out of curiosity, while writing this chapter, I googled the search term 'Jennifer Anniston children' and was presented with over 40 million search results! Page one alone brought up articles about Anniston 'sensationally defending herself for not having children' and 'being hounded by pregnancy rumours for decades'.

In one interview, Anniston says: 'I don't like [the pressure] that people put on me, on women – that you've failed yourself as a female because you haven't procreated. I don't think it's fair. You may not have a child come out of your vagina, but that doesn't mean you aren't mothering – dogs, friends, friends' children.'[1]

It is unfathomable to me that one of the most famous actresses of our time, someone who works incredibly hard and is successful in so many ways, has to constantly defend her child-free status. And she's just one very public example of what women have to face when they don't have children.

Of course, let's be honest, even women who do have children are not immune to societal judgements.

Let's think about the stereotypes...

Working mothers are ambitious, driven and absent from their children's lives.

Stay at home mothers are lazy, unproductive and do not contribute to society.

We're basically damned if we do, damned if we don't, and damned for however we do it.

I actually find this realisation quite liberating because it means that the best we can all do is make the decisions that are right for us in terms of motherhood, rather than worrying what anyone else expects of us.

I foam at the mouth with anger when people feel entitled to comment on women's bodies and whether or not they have children. There's no way of knowing who is dealing with illness, multiple miscarriages, infertility, relationship difficulties, past bereavement, financial difficulties, circumstances not being right or simply not wanting to become a parent.

I think the world would be a much better place if we could just all mind our own business and be kind!

Overcoming the guilt and turmoil

Something a lot of women I know have struggled with is the desire to be seen as more than 'just a mum'. Because women are so often defined in terms of our role (or not) as a mother, we can end up feeling stripped of our identity.

But, as we'll see throughout this book, there is a huge amount of pressure on women to make motherhood the be-all-and-end-all of our existence, even if it doesn't feel like the right thing to do personally.

I would never, ever, put down or diminish stay at home mums but, for me, I always knew I wanted to continue to work after having children. I also knew I wanted to do it in a way that let me attend assemblies, sports day, performances, etc. and still give me and my family financial security.

Building my own businesses helped me to achieve this.

That's not to say I was immune to the guilt and turmoil that comes with being a working mum! Oh no, I certainly wrestled with those feelings for a long time.

What the research says

Something that helped me overcome the dreaded mum guilt was to look at what research says about us working mums. I know I probably shouldn't have cared – after all, I had to do what was right for me and my family – but I did often wonder if societal expectations were fair.

Should I be going back to work?

Would my children be OK with a working mum or would they miss out?

Actually, the research is pretty reassuring.

One major study from Harvard Business School by Professor Kathleen McGinn (2015)[2] found that:

*   Children of working mums grow up to be just as happy as children of stay at home mums

*   Daughters of employed mothers across 29 different countries were 1.21 times more likely to be employed and 1.29 times more likely to supervise others

*   They are also higher paid, earning an average of $1,880 more per year than daughters of mums who'd stayed at home

*   Men who grew up with working mums tend to devote an extra 50 minutes per week caring for their family and carrying out household chores, seeing a better division of labour between men and women

*   Working mothers provide positive role models for both boys and girls, and their children tend to grow up with a much more equal view of gender in the workplace

*   Children of working mothers tend to stay in education for longer

Another study called 'When Does Time Matter? Maternal Employment, Children's Time With Parents, and Child Development'[3] concluded that, while working mums spend fewer hours with their children, they actually spend more quality time with them than stay at home mums. This can be directly linked to a 0.03 to 0.04 SD (stand deviation) improvement to cognitive development.

A study in Denmark[4] found that the children who perform best academically are those whose mums work between 10 and 19 hours a week, rather than working full-time or staying at home. This suggests some advantages to the middle ground where we mums can be with our kids to support their learning and development but be a working role model.

Now, of course, I imagine that if I had wanted to be a stay at home mum, I could have easily found research to support this decision too.

For example, a 2014 study by Eric Bettinger, associate professor at Stanford School of Education, using data from Norway, found that older children perform better academically if they have a stay at home parent (not necessarily mum)[5]. This is because the parent can influence how the child spends their time and help guide academic activities whereas in many families where both parents work, older children spend a lot of time in front of the TV or a games console.

My point here is that there is research to support almost any position relating to mums and whether or not we work.

I'll say it again, the only choice is to do what feels right for you.

It's OK to focus on you!

I am so proud of being a self-employed mum. While it isn't the right choice for everyone, all I can tell you is that it is absolutely the right choice for me.

I love that my girls see me as a role model (their words, not mine) and they are already absorbing entrepreneurial skills just by being around me. I love that they see me as being in charge of my own finances and that they will be good custodians of money in the future. They already know that half of any money they receive is to be spent and the other half goes into the bank for rainy days!

It's so important to me that my children see me putting my needs high on my list for a life well-lived. I don't want them to compromise themselves in the future or to put themselves to the bottom of their list, so I want them to see that you can be a loving, lovable, amazing woman and still prioritise yourself.

Some of you might recoil in horror when I say that I expect the girls to do chores around the house or make their own meals sometimes rather than doing everything myself, but I believe that by fostering essential life skills now, they'll be much more prepared for adult life. And isn't that my job as their mum? To help them be confident, happy, functioning adults when the time comes.

The research backs me up on this.

A study by Marty Rossmann at the University of Minnesota found that involving children in household tasks from an early age has a positive impact later in life[6]. Giving children age-appropriate chores to do around the house increases their sense of responsibility, competence, self-reliance and self-worth throughout their lives.

What I'm saying here is that you don't have to do everything for everyone in your family.

You might feel like you have to be ever available because things will fall apart without you. Trust me, they won't. Everyone will survive; they may even thrive.

Back in 2016, the Trend Report by Vistaprint found that 72% of female micro-business owners had seen an improvement in their family life as a direct result of their entrepreneurship[7].

If you want to work, step up in your career, run a business, spend time on a hobby etc, it's OK to prioritise those things. Your children won't suffer.

In fact, they may gain a great deal from seeing their mum embracing her potential.

Becoming a mum is a wonderful thing if it's what you want in life. But if or when you do become a mum, it doesn't have to become your entire identity (unless, of course, you want it to).

I want my girls to look at me and what I've been able to achieve in life and use that as their yardstick. I want them to think, 'If mum could do that, then I can do it too. In fact, I could do more'.

By moving myself right up to the top of my list of priorities, I actually think I am setting my daughters up for success too. Talk about win-win.

A car can run on fumes for so long but it needs to be refuelled or it will stop running altogether.

You as a mother can't continue to be everything to everybody. Eventually you will break down.

You need to make time for yourself, to rejuvenate, to make sure YOU are not lost while trying to hold everything together.

-@sayhellofreedom

REFLECTION TIME

How do you feel?

_____

_____

_____

What have you learnt?

_____

_____

_____

What will you change?

_____

_____

_____

What will you do more of?

_____

_____

_____

What will you do less of?

_____

_____

_____

Does this raise any strong feelings for you?
(This is your gut telling you that there's a potential issue you need to address)

_____

_____

_____

Do you have any questions?

_____

_____

_____

Chapter 4:

Dreams vs Reality

(Whose dreams are you living and what would
you do if you were guaranteed to succeed?)

When I talk about dreams, I don't mean the flying, naked in public, teeth falling out variety that help our brains process the day when we're asleep.

No, dreams, in the context of this book, are the things that you would love to achieve and experience during your lifetime.

Most people have dreams in life. They can be big or small, shared or completely unique. Whatever they are though, they should drive us forward. They should motivate us and give life purpose and meaning.

Some people dream of being famous, others of retiring at 40. There are those who want to travel the globe, while others dream of putting down roots. Some want a houseful of children, others a houseful of rescue animals.

Your dreams might include a list of places you want to visit or adventures you want to experience. Maybe you dream of running a marathon or writing a bestseller. Or is a fire walk or solo skydive a dream that inspires you?

Everyone's dreams are different.

But whatever our dreams, they're an important part of our identities. They tell us a lot about our values and how we would choose to live, all things being equal. They give us something to strive towards, goals that can shape our decisions and help us to grow.

Personally, I think having dreams is at the heart of being human. Dreams represent hope, potential, satisfaction and fulfilment. They are the very essence of our individuality.

What are your dreams?

If I were to ask you right now what your dreams are, would you be able to tell me?

For some people, it's an easy question because their dreams are always present. For others though, this question can be really tough.

Sometimes, we forget to dream. Sometimes, we lose sight of our dreams or become cynical. Sometimes, our reality feels so far away from our dreams that it's easier to let go of our dreams all together.

But as I've mentioned before, tapping into your dreams can be a powerful way to reconnect with what really matters to you and what gives your life deeper meaning.

In this chapter, I want to help you name and claim your dreams.

When a dose of 'reality' is the killer of dreams

If you can name your dreams, do you feel like they're at odds with your reality? That they're an either/or kind of thing rather than able to coexist harmoniously?

Did you dream your life would take you somewhere completely different to where you are right now? And, if so, how does that make you feel?

On the other hand, you might be the person whose life looks exactly as you imagined it – on paper at least – and yet something still doesn't feel quite right. It could be a big or a little thing that feels off.

The issue of striving for our dreams versus accepting our reality is a tricky one, and there are good reasons for that.

Our society is packed full of contradictions. It tells us to pursue our dreams no matter what, often presenting the have-it-all lifestyle as an easy, overnight achievement and the pinnacle of what we should all be aiming for. And if we don't pursue our dreams, we can be made to feel like we're lagging behind or missing out on some secret of success that everyone else is in on.

At the same time, we're told that 'you mustn't get too big for your boots', 'don't dream too big', 'who do you think you are?' or 'stay in your lane'. There's pressure to rein it back in and play it small, so you don't stand out from the norm.

People often talk about dreams being for the young, as though you only have one opportunity to set a course in life and then it's gone. This can especially be the case as you accumulate responsibility, a partner, a mortgage, children. How can you possibly do XYZ when you have to think of 123? I'm sure you can fill in the blanks from your own experiences.

But if you think about it, even children can have their dreams squashed before they've really formed. Just as people from an early age can inspire you to dream big and reach for the stars, people can also consciously or subconsciously do the opposite.

Parents push their kids with their own beliefs: 'Only the best athletes succeed but I think you'd make a great engineer'. Careers advisors can stop dreams in their tracks: 'You have to get straight As to study medicine but you're very good at English so maybe you should do that at uni instead?' Even teachers can diminish dreams before they have a chance to take hold: 'You're not a natural artist', 'You're too big to be a dancer' or 'That's not a real career'.

As a salon owner, I see more and more people wanting to follow their passion and train in hairdressing or beauty later on in life because they were talked out of it when they were younger, pushed into something else by their parents or teachers.

The fact is that 'you're never too old to dream' but, practically speaking, dreams can be harder to achieve when you're older, especially if you have other people and responsibilities to consider (think partner, kids, ageing parents, business partners).

Your dreams or theirs?

As we get older, many of us end up feeling like we have to 'give in' to a reality we haven't planned, conditioned to be grateful for our lot and, in doing so, sacrifice our dreams. This is especially the case if you're living your life based on what other people expect of you (more about this in Chapter 8). A by-product of this is that we can end up taking on dreams that don't truly belong to us.

It can be hard to spot that we're doing this. If you've always been told you should want something, it can become so deeply ingrained that it takes a long time to realise it isn't necessarily what you really want.

Then there's the question of how much of your life and attention you should devote to your dreams.

It's a difficult balancing act. If you focus too much on your dreams, you can miss what's happening in reality right now.

But, on the other hand, to live without dreams seems like half a life.

Everyone struggles

I think most of us believed when we were younger, that life would get easier as we got older. When we looked to our adult selves, we saw a future carved out of realised dreams.

We envisioned a life of no-one telling us what we could and couldn't do. We thought we would be able to make our own decisions with no repercussions – it might be what time we come home at night, our dream job, the 'perfect' family set up or simply the opportunity to have hot cookie dough and chocolate ice cream for breakfast, lunch and dinner, (OK, that last one might just be me).

However, the truth is that many of us struggle to balance our dreams with reality. We get further into adulthood and yet things might not work out how we imagined them. Our dreams don't always move closer into reality.

Fortunately, this distance between dreams and reality doesn't have to be permanent.

It starts with accepting reality and making it your starting point

When people talk about accepting reality, it's often with an implied message that we should surrender and let go of our dreams. Or that reality is, by default, unsatisfying.

I think this is the wrong outlook.

Acceptance doesn't mean resignation or surrender.

It doesn't mean passively letting life push us, rudderless, from pillar to post. It's not about quitting or lowering the bar on what we want from life.

Instead, accepting reality is about no longer fighting the things that you have no control over (more about that in Chapter 11). It's also about recognising and feeling gratitude for the many wonderful things in our lives as they are today.

If you do have unfulfilled dreams, you'll need to examine them and focus on what you can do to make them happen, starting right now. Because, while you can't change other people or live for their expectations, you can change yourself and ask things of your potential.

But how can we each achieve this?

The key is to pinpoint what you have the power to change, why you want to change it and then take action to make those specific changes.

For example, maybe your reality is that you have young children and you want to launch a business but can only work on it part-time right now. You can't actively change this, but you can develop ways to make the most of your work time, for example, outsourcing, automation, planning, etc. to move your business dreams forward in small steps.

If you lay the groundwork now, your business can grow alongside your children. And that's OK, by accepting that your children won't be this young forever, it becomes easier to enjoy your journey, where they and your business are right now, rather than wishing the time away.

Be honest about your dreams

My first piece of advice is to take an honest look at your dreams.

It can be tough but try to ask yourself why the life you dream of is so important to you?

For example, are your dreams your own?

On your deathbed, do you think you'd regret not achieving a specific dream? I know that if someone else had opened a salon with a crèche and I hadn't, I would have regretted it right until my last moment.

Do you expect your life to look a certain way because other people have told you that's what you should want or do your dreams reflect what you truly desire?

As with living up to other people's expectations, a lot of getting to the truth about this comes down to 'gut' feeling. If, for example, you have everything you thought you ever wanted but you still don't feel a sense of accomplishment, then maybe you've been striving for something that doesn't come from within. Or maybe you just haven't taken time to take stock and celebrate what you've achieved?

If aspects of your dreams feel uncomfortable or at odds with who you are, they may no longer serve you. Equally, if your dreams light you up inside, if they make you feel passionate and excited, then they deserve to be heard.

If your dreams are truly rooted inside of you then what can you do to make them your reality, one step at a time, while accepting the reality of where you are today?

Take control of your life

Accepting your reality while keeping your dreams alive comes down to taking control of what you can and letting go of what you can't.

Make conscious decisions and take conscious action.

Try framing everything within the question, if I do this, will it take me closer to my dreams or further away from them?

Also ask yourself, is this something that I have the power to change? If so, what must I do to achieve a different outcome?

Dreams play such an important role. They give us waypoints to navigate towards on this journey through life. They offer a route map.

If we listen to our dreams and we follow them properly, they give us control over our journey. They make life something that happens for us, not to us.

Dreams can change

But sometimes our destination will change, or we'll want to take a different route. This is why it's important to revisit your dreams often.

What you dreamed about as a child may not reflect the dreams you have now. On the other hand, maybe the core truth of your dreams has never changed.

Dancers, actors, singers and artists often talk about how they've only ever wanted to create or perform. I knew I wanted to be an author from the first time I read a Roald Dahl book, it just took me 36 years to do it!

For others, dreams can change. I often speak to women whose dreams for their romantic relationships or how they parent their children have changed. Some have new dreams for their careers or how they spend their spare time.

It makes sense to me that as we learn and grow as people our dreams can evolve with us.

I also believe, however, that we can wish away our lives in the pursuit of dreams. This is why I'm a big fan of learning to live in the moment. If we can feel good about today, as clichéd as it may sound, it can only fuel a better tomorrow.

Dreams and reality can coexist. You just have to take charge of both.

Activity Two: Dare to Dream

Again, I want you to find ten minutes in your day when you won't be interrupted. As with Activity One, there's no judgement here if you need to lock yourself in the bathroom, sneak out to your car or plonk the kids in front of an electronic babysitter to achieve this!

Now, I want you to set a timer on your phone for ten minutes and hit 'Start' when I say to.

For these ten minutes, I want you to use the template overleaf and write down everything you can about your dreams for the future. The most important thing is to write down what your dreams would look like if you were guaranteed their success.

Try not to overthink. I especially want you to ignore what other people might think or what other people might want for you. These are YOUR dreams. What would they look like if you knew you couldn't fail? What would you do? Who would you be?

Now press 'Start' on that timer and off you go... You've got this!

My Dreams...

REFLECTION TIME

How do you feel?

_____

_____

_____

What have you learnt?

_____

_____

_____

What will you change?

_____

_____

_____

What will you do more of?

_____

_____

_____

What will you do less of?

_____

_____

_____

Does this raise any strong feelings for you?
(This is your gut telling you that there's a potential issue you need to address)

_____

_____

_____

Do you have any questions?

_____

_____

_____

Chapter 5:

Limiting beliefs

(Unpack the emotional baggage you're carrying
and the unkind things you say to yourself)

Having identified your dreams, or at least got you thinking about what they might be, I want you to take a look at the thoughts that might try to sabotage you or the thoughts that tell you you're not worth prioritising. These thoughts are called 'limiting beliefs'.

In this chapter, you're going to learn how to spot a limiting belief, how to challenge it and how to replace it with an empowering belief. It's a pretty meaty chapter so do your best to stick with it, if you can get through it start to finish, well done. It is also understanable to move on with the book if you get stuck, you can always come back to it later.

What are 'limiting beliefs'?

A limiting belief is something you believe to be true that holds you back or restricts you in some way. You can have limiting beliefs about yourself, other people or the world.

What limiting beliefs are you holding on to?

In case you're not sure, I've put together a list of examples for you. Do any of them sound familiar?

There are so many more limiting beliefs that I could have added to this list - beliefs that I have seen and heard over the years that hold wonderful women back. Although they're equally as important, quite frankly, I could write a whole book devoted to them and we need to get on with this one!

Do any of these beliefs strike a chord with you? I could certainly of ticked a few off myself in the past and maybe still a couple today.

List of limiting beliefs I've come across

I am not good at running

I am not fit

I am not healthy

I will never be skinny/slim/healthy

I am shy

I am loud

I am too much for people

I am not good enough

I am not clever enough

I am not pretty

I am too pretty

I am not funny

No-one gets my sense of humour

Everyone else is more important than me

I cannot make the same amount of money that other people are making

I do not know my worth

I am needy

I will let people walk all over me

My opinion isn't worthwhile

I am too old

I am too young

I have the worst luck in the world

I am just lucky

I am not important

I am selfish if I say no

I am too opinionated

I am not opinionated enough

It's easier for everyone else

I am a victim

I have to do everything myself

I only trust myself

Being vunerable is weak

I cannot charge my worth

It is safer in my comfort zone

I don't make good decisions

Everyone expects me to make the decisions

I am a control freak

I feel so out of control

I can't change

Change scares me

I fail at everything

I can never finish what I started

I am too emotional

I am not emotional enough

You can't have it all

I am unemployable

I am undateable

People take my kindness for weakness

Everyone lets me down in the end

I should be happy with my lot

If I can't do this, I can't do that

I'll only ever fail so why even try

I'm never happy

I have low expectations

I have high expectations

I'm too friendly

I care too much about what people think

I don't care what people think of me

I don't fit in

I have a resting bitch face

There's no such thing as a perfect life

Where do limiting beliefs come from?

'Your brain is like Velcro for negative experiences and Teflon for positive ones, even though most of your experiences are probably positive or neutral.' – Dr Rick Hanson

Limiting beliefs can develop in many different ways. They can come from things other people have said or experiences that have shaped how you see yourself and your place in the world.

Often, limiting beliefs can disguise themselves as being helpful or protecting you in some way, for example, 'you're not good enough to charge that so don't embarrass yourself by trying' or 'all relationships end badly so it's better not to get involved with anyone'.

They can even show up in everyday situations like not going on the trampoline with your kids ('I'm too old/overweight/unfit or I'll make a fool of myself') or striking up a conversation with the other mums at the park ('They might not like me, what if she thinks I'm a weirdo for trying to start a conversation?').

But instead of protecting you, all these limiting beliefs really do is hold you back by affecting your behaviours. Not only do they affect us personally but they can start affecting other people too.

How limiting beliefs show up

It isn't always easy to recognise our limiting beliefs, especially if this is the first time you've come across the term. Hopefully, after reading this chapter you'll be more aware of them and how they show up in day-to-day life, preventing you from moving forward or doing something you really want to do.

It might help to keep in mind that limiting beliefs tend to show up in certain scenarios, for example, when you:

* Make excuses

* Complain about things

* Have negative thoughts

* Indulge in unhelpful habits

* Talk to yourself in limiting and unhelpful ways

* Jump to conclusions and/or make assumptions

* Procrastinate

* Try to be perfect

Can you identify with any of those? I know I'm definitely guilty of all of the above, especially when I feel out of my comfort zone or my confidence is lacking. In fact, many of them showed up writing this book!

Pay attention to resistance

Are there times when you feel resistance internally while setting a goal? You might have felt it when I asked you to write down your dreams in Activity Two. This resistance is often a sign of a limiting belief.

One example of this shows up daily with many of the female entrepreneurs that I work with – the internal struggle with pricing their services.

Someone might say, 'I want to earn £50 an hour' or '£100,000 a year' or 'I want to charge £3,000 for my VIP coaching service', but the limiting beliefs will quickly kick in.

The push-back is almost instant.

Who am I to think I can charge that? There's no way people will pay that much to work with me. I'm not worth that much. I mustn't be greedy. I should probably charge £30 an hour instead. I just need enough to cover the bills.

Every one of these statements is the sign of a limiting belief.

I've even experienced female clients having a mini meltdown at the suggestion of increasing their price by £1. Yes, really!

These thoughts, whatever they are for you, indicate the presence of limiting beliefs around self-worth, value, wealth, abundance and more.

The good thing is you can learn to challenge your limiting beliefs and stop them from holding you back once and for all.

Why we need to challenge our limiting beliefs

Limiting beliefs can prevent us from doing things we want to or being the person we really want to be. They can also make us continue to do things that we know aren't beneficial or healthy for us either.

More often than not, limiting beliefs stop us from moving forward in life, even when we want or need to more than anything else in the world.

As we've seen, there is a wide range of limiting beliefs that people hold on to. They could be about themselves or about different things like other people, ambitions, capabilities, permissions, situations, opportunities, judgements, money, relationships, emotions... The list really does go on and on and on, but you get the picture.

Whatever your limiting beliefs are, whether you have one or one hundred, I can pretty much guarantee that not a single one is useful to you, especially if you are wanting to grow as a person and make changes. In fact, each belief is probably as debilitating as it is frustrating.

Activity Three: Recognising your limiting beliefs

With this in mind, the next thing I want you to do is to write down all the things you think you can't do, i.e. everything you think you're 'no good at'. Let everything that's holding you back spill out onto the page. All of the negative things you tell yourself, all of the things you do when you don't want to and all of the things you don't do because the voice in your head tells you, you can't. Write down all of the things that you know are stopping you from growing and trying out new things or that are preventing you from putting yourself out there.

This will be completely personal to you. Every single person that does this activity will have different answers and beliefs, and that's just fine. Everyone has a different story and experiences that lead them to where they are now, holding on to their limiting beliefs.

This exercise can make you feel vulnerable and some people struggle to get started. If you're stuck, have a read through the list I provided and jot down any of the beliefs that resonate (it's like Limiting Belief Bingo!).

Now it's your turn. Give yourself ten minutes (you can set that handy timer again to keep you focused) to jot down all the limiting beliefs that hang out in your head. Again, try not to overthink or censor what you write.

You can use the space over the page or print out a worksheet at:

https://www.jobevilacqua.com/resources/

LIMITING BELIEFS

What are your limiting beliefs?

Write down all the things that you know stop you from growing, trying out new things, or prevent you from putting yourself out there.

_____

_____

_____

_____

_____

_____

_____

_____

_____

_____

_____

_____

_____

_____

_____

_____

_____

_____

_____

_____

_____

_____

Our limitations and success will be based, most often, on our own expectations for ourselves.

What the mind dwells upon, the body acts upon.

- Denis Waitley

Spotting the language of limiting beliefs

Looking at the list of limiting beliefs that you've just written, I bet that certain words have come up time and again.

It can be really helpful to be able to spot the language we usually use to express a limiting belief because then you can challenge it.

Look for the following words in your list from Activity Three:

* I do/don't

E.g. I do everything and it's not good enough, I don't deserve it, I don't know how to...

These beliefs often hold us back from expecting or seeking out good things.

* I can /can't

E.g. I can only work for someone else, I can't draw, I can't speak in public...

These beliefs usually tell us that our skills are fixed and that we're unable to learn something new.

* I must/mustn't

E.g. I must clean the house every day, I must make sure the kids do lots of extra-curricular activities, I mustn't be lazy by having a lie-in...

Society is built on certain values, norms, laws and rules but not every belief we have is mandatory. Sometimes the beliefs that we have about what we must and must not do stop us from using our time to do something that brings us pleasure.

* I should/shouldn't

E.g. I should always give the kids home-cooked meals, I shouldn't ask for too much money, I should make more of an effort with my appearance...

Should/shouldn't limiting beliefs often come from other people and the weight of their expectations. These beliefs are about how to think, feel or behave based on what people will think of you if they were looking in from the outside.

* I am/am not

E.g. I am stupid, I am fat, I am ugly, I am not good enough...

These beliefs tend to suggest that how we are is fixed and that change is not possible. We use them to define ourselves in very black and white terms. Even seemingly positive statements such as 'I am a mathematician' come with an implied downside '...so I'm not creative or good with my hands'. There's something absolute about these beliefs. A statement like 'I am stupid' encompasses your entire being rather than something more forgiving like, 'That was a stupid thing to do but I can learn from it'.

* Others are/will

E.g. Others are more capable than me, Others know more than me, Others will not like me...

Just as we have limiting beliefs about ourselves, we also have beliefs about other people that limit us too. For example, if you believe other people are more capable or more intelligent than you, then you may not feel able to challenge them, even when you know they're wrong.

We often try to guess or assume we know what others think and feel or how they will behave towards us based on our assumptions, beliefs and previous experiences.

*   How the world works (is/are/will/always)

E.g. Dogs will bite, Air travel is dangerous, People in my city are too busy to make new friends...

Again, these limiting beliefs tend to come both from other people's opinions and our lived experiences. They're typically all or nothing in nature, generalising what you can expect from the world, e.g. That person was unfriendly therefore all people here are unfriendly or that cat scratched me so all cats will scratch me.

Can you see how limiting beliefs tend to use very black or white language, seeing something as absolute rather than flexible? It's time to start challenging what's holding you back.

Activity Four: Find the source of your limiting beliefs

Let's go back to the list of limiting beliefs that you wrote down in Activity Three.

Next to each limiting belief, I want you to acknowledge where it has come from.

Was it from your childhood, your parents, a teacher, a partner, an ex-partner, a friend, someone at work, from a situation where you got hurt (emotionally or physically), from a story you read in the newspaper or a magazine, or something that you assume?

Again, there is no judgement here. Try to acknowledge the belief and recognise where you first heard it. This isn't about placing blame. This exercise will help you see that limiting beliefs come from all sorts of places but that this doesn't make them gospel.

You can use the space over the page or print out a worksheet at: https://www.jobevilacqua.com/resources/

LIMITING BELIEFS

Next to each limiting belief, acknowledge where it has come from.

Limiting Belief	Reason

Challenging your limiting beliefs

When you notice a limiting belief rearing its unhelpful head, try to take a moment to acknowledge it by asking yourself three questions:

1.   Where does this belief come from? (Refer back to Activity Four if you need a reminder)

2.   What has made me hold on to this belief for so long?

3.   What specific experiences have supported this belief?

With questions two and three, you will need to think about all the times something or someone has reinforced a limiting belief. For example, maybe you see yourself as being clumsy or unsporty. This belief may have started when you fell over in front of everyone during a PE lesson or when you came last in a Sports Day race; it may even have been when you were picked last for a team game at school (anyone else remember that horror?). Holding on to this belief has protected you from physical injury or embarrassment. Every time you feel out of breath or avoid exercise, it reinforces your belief.

But the same belief could also mean that your health is suffering. While you could live and play hard without exercising or eating well a few years ago and still feel great, you're starting to notice aches and pains that make you think you need to start taking better care of yourself.

As we can see, while your limiting beliefs have a good intention – i.e. to protect you from short-term, immediate discomfort – they may actually be causing you more pain in the long-term. This means that despite the reason they came about, they're no longer serving you.

So, how can you let them go?

We're going to dive straight into another activity.

Activity Five: Smashing your limiting beliefs

The only way to break free of a limiting belief is to challenge its logic and realise it doesn't serve you positively. At first, you will need to do this consciously, questioning your beliefs time and again.

This process can be broken down into four stages that explore:

1.   What the limiting belief feels like now and whether you're actually getting anything good from holding on to it

2.   How a limiting belief is affecting your ability to pursue your dreams

3.   Highlighting all the ways in which a limiting belief is holding you back and why it needs to be smashed

4.   Acknowledging what your life will look like with or without each limiting belief

I've put together some great questions that can help you to move through these stages. You will find them over the page. I appreciate that this is one of the bigger exercises so pick one limiting belief at a time and work your way through the questions (you will find more copies of the worksheet at: https://www.jobevilacqua.com/resources/.) You might need to pause between each stage to reflect on your answers. There's no rush here.

Remember to come back to this activity every time you notice a limiting belief. With practice, you will learn how to challenge your beliefs without having to write everything down.

For now, try to allow 20 minutes to really dig deep into smashing a limiting belief. Use that phone timer to keep you focused.

Over to you.

SMASHING YOUR LIMITING BELIEFS

Stage one: Name your limiting belief and how it makes you feel.

How am I deriving pleasure or something good by holding on to this limiting belief? (The chances are you're not!)

_____

_____

_____

What value am I gaining from holding on to this limiting belief?

_____

_____

_____

If I picture my limiting belief as an object, what does it look like?

_____

_____

_____

If I picture my limiting belief as an object, what is it like? Describe what it looks, sounds, tastes, smells and feels like.

_____

_____

_____

Stage two: Think about the dreams you wrote down in Activity Two (Chapter 4). How are your limiting beliefs holding you back from achieving them?

Name one of your dreams. When you think about it, what limiting beliefs pop into your mind? These will be the reasons you tell yourself that you can't do something. Write down everything you can about your limiting beliefs surrounding your chosen dream.
(You might notice different limiting beliefs for different goals).

Stage three: Challenge the truth of your limiting belief (remember, just pick one belief for now).

Is this belief accurate?

_____

_____

_____

If a friend told me they believed this, what would I say to them?

_____

_____

_____

Was there a time when I didn't believe this? Why, and what changed?

_____

_____

_____

What evidence shows that my limiting belief is wrong?

_____

_____

_____

What is the exact opposite of this belief?

_____

_____

_____

What is funny, silly, strange or embarrassing about this belief?

_____

_____

_____

Is this belief helping me get what I want in life?

_____

_____

_____

Would other people think that this belief is correct?

_____

_____

_____

How would thinking the opposite of this belief help me?

_____

_____

_____

Are there any famous or inspirational quotes that throw doubt on my limiting belief?

_____

_____

_____

How would I think about this belief if I were a successful entrepreneur/Albert Einstein/The Queen/a child/a dog/an elephant/my best friend? With this question, you can insert any example you want and make it as off-the-wall as you like. The idea is to remind your brain that perspective, context and personal experience change our beliefs.

_____

_____

_____

Stage four: Recognise the potential consequences of hanging on to your limiting beliefs.

What will your life look like if you hang on to your limiting beliefs?

_____

_____

_____

How will this belief affect you emotionally, physically, spiritually, financially or in your relationships with others?

_____

_____

_____

How does it make you feel when you think of always having this limiting belief?

_____

_____

_____

Why is it important to make a change now?

_____

_____

_____

The point of Activity Five is not to upset you or make you feel silly, but the more you recognise the limitations of holding on to a belief, the more you will feel motivated to make a positive change.

A crucial part of letting go of your limiting beliefs is finding new beliefs to replace them. You need guiding principles that are going to empower you and drive you on towards your goals instead of holding you back.

Knowing this, we're going to strike while the iron is hot and move straight into the next activity.

Activity Six: Finding your empowering beliefs

I want you to picture yourself as the person you would like to grow into, free from your limiting beliefs. Think about what you would like to achieve, the values you want to uphold and how you would like to see yourself, your true self.

I've included some questions as prompts. You can use the space over the page or print out a worksheet at:

https://www.jobevilacqua.com/resources/

EMPOWERING BELIEFS

Answer the questions below as though you were talking about your future self, the truest, happiest self:

What would this person like to achieve in life?

_____

_____

_____

What would this person believe about themselves while in pursuit of this goal?

_____

_____

_____

What would this person believe about themselves in general?

_____

_____

_____

How does this person think about their goal and how does this affect their attitude to life?

_____

_____

_____

How would they think about obstacles between them and their goal?

_____

_____

_____

What would this person believe after achieving their goal?

_____

_____

_____

I would now like you to apply your answers to yourself and how it would feel to claim those beliefs and thoughts as your own. Pick one positive, empowering new belief from your notes.

What are the benefits of this new belief?

_____

_____

_____

How will this new belief help you reach your goals?

_____

_____

_____

How will this new belief change your life for the better?

_____

_____

_____

How will this belief help you in the short and long-term?

_____

_____

_____

How will this belief make you feel about yourself?

_____

_____

_____

To what extent will this belief empower you to make a change?

_____

_____

_____

Why is this belief important to you?

_____

_____

_____

Practising your new empowering beliefs

Our limiting beliefs won't go away overnight (if only!), especially if they've been hanging around for years.

On the plus side, we get good at what we practice, which is why I'm going to urge you to start consciously practising your new empowering beliefs.

How?

Think about whether there are any habits or behaviours that would support your new beliefs. If there are, start implementing them and tick them off on a chart every day to show your progress.

Are there any famous or inspirational quotes that echo what you want to believe? If so, write them down and carry them with you to read as often as possible throughout the day.

Are there any people, news stories, fictional stories, slogans or symbols that reflect your new beliefs? Read them, read about them, print off pictures of them, and write about them often!

The aim is to collect as much evidence as possible that supports your new empowering beliefs. The more evidence your brain sees, the stronger your new beliefs will become (and the weaker your old limiting beliefs will be).

Every day, try to take small steps to reinforce your new thinking. Many people love tools like bullet journals where they highlight each time they perform a new habit or write down every positive decision.

When you're embedding a new belief, everything needs to be very deliberate and conscious because your brain is practising something new. It takes time for new networks to form, consistency is key here.

Keep going and you will gradually bring the 'true you' from your imagination into the physical world - a true you no longer trapped by limiting beliefs.

REFLECTION TIME

How do you feel?

_____

_____

_____

What have you learnt?

_____

_____

_____

What will you change?

_____

_____

_____

What will you do more of?

_____

_____

_____

What will you do less of?

_____

_____

_____

Does this raise any strong feelings for you?
(This is your gut telling you that there's a potential issue you need to address)

_____

_____

_____

Do you have any questions?

_____

_____

_____

Don't let a bad
day
make you feel like
you have a bad life

- Unknown

Chapter 6:

Are you trapped?

(Taking back control in areas where feel like you have none)

Have you ever felt trapped in your life, whether in the past or even right now?

It could be that there's one small area where you feel stuck or maybe you would change some pretty big things given half a chance.

I'm not just talking about being physically trapped here; humans can be emotionally and/or financially trapped too. The latter is not often talked about but it's something that I'm really passionate about eradicating.

Growing up, I saw a lot of women staying in relationships because they were financially trapped. It's something that I experienced at 21, even though for years I vowed it would never happen to me. I know from experience how a lack of money can make you feel like you have limited opportunities and options.

Being financially trapped can show up in different ways. Are you living hand to mouth with nothing to spare at the end of every month because of the astronomical interest you're paying on old debts?

Do you earn enough to pay the bills but you're never able to get ahead or splurge on anything extra, like a break away from your usual four walls?

Or, worst-case scenario, are you being financially controlled by a partner and have to ask for permission before you buy anything? Or are you conditioned to believe you couldn't support you or your family alone without your partner's income?

The saying goes that money can't buy you happiness and I agree, but I certainly believe that it can buy us more options in life.

A survey by VoucherCodesPro in 2017 found that 64% of women have to switch jobs after they have children for more flexibility to cover childcare but, in doing so, have to take a salary drop of £11,000 in the process[8]. A change in financial circumstances like this can have a huge impact on your choices.

Even not having enough expendable income to invest in your own personal growth and development can make you feel like your options are limited and you are trapped in the here and now, without the ability to keep moving forward. It can be as frustrating as it can be debilitating.

Then there are the emotional reasons that you might feel trapped: a sense of loyalty, low confidence, relationships and patterns of behaviour from your family and friends, spending years building a career and believing that it's too late to walk away.

All of these things – and many more – can make you feel like you have no choice but to accept elements of your life where you feel unfulfilled.

Let's look at these common 'traps' in a bit more detail – ones that I've been in myself or friends or clients have been in. Maybe one or many will resonate with you.

There are some women who are unhappy in their romantic relationships but are trapped emotionally and/or financially. They believe they can't afford to leave their partner or that it's too late to find anyone else in life.

Then there are others who are feeling trapped in another way, separate to their healthy, happy relationships.

Perhaps you've always wanted to work for yourself, but you're trapped by needing a guaranteed monthly income?

Maybe you'd give anything to change career but having spent many years getting to where you are now, it seems crazy to change paths at this stage in life? I mean, what about the drop in income or status for a start?

You could even feel trapped by small domestic duties. Maybe you'd love to go for a run when the kids go to bed but you believe that a 'good' mum would need to read a bedtime story to them every single evening so you rule out using this time differently.

Or perhaps you'd love to spend your weekends pursuing a hobby but instead you find yourself in a never-ending cycle of catching up on the washing, food shopping, cleaning and taking your kids to their extra-curricular activities.

As we can see, there are so many different ways that, as women, we can come to feel trapped.

Recognising that you feel trapped

It can be surprisingly hard to recognise or admit that you feel trapped by something in your life. And, of course, it can be even harder to decide to do something about it. Many people live their whole lives believing 'This is just the way things are and I need to accept that', but is this really how you want to live?

The way I see it, we each only get one shot at this thing called life. Why spend even part of it in a metaphorical cage?

The things we've covered already are quite specific and not everyone reading them will resonate, so I want to cover some generic signs that you might be feeling trapped right now.

Maybe one of these strikes a chord with you?

1.   You don't like your job

Hey, we've all done jobs that we don't like before, but this usually happens during a transitory phase in life, such as moving from education into a career. A more worrying sign of feeling trapped is when you're in the career that you've worked towards and you feel like it's a bad fit. If the bad days are outweighing the good at work, it might be a sign that it's time for a career change.

2.   You're withdrawn

If you find that you're spending more time away from your friends or family because you can't see another option, then this is a clue that you might be feeling trapped. Many people withdraw from life when they don't want to be reminded about the reality they're living.

3.   You don't have a support system

Often, a side effect of withdrawing from a life you feel trapped in is that you withdraw from your potential support system too. Or it could be that you don't have a good support system with your current circle of friends or family and that's part of why you feel trapped.

4.   You always feel restless

Another sign of feeling trapped is a sense of restlessness. Do you always feel like you have to be busy doing something? Does the thought of sitting still horrify you? Maybe you always have what can only be described as a 'great dissatisfaction', like something is wrong in life but you don't know what. Keeping busy can help you to avoid confronting your feelings.

5.   You lie about your life (or perhaps embellish the details)

Are you someone who always posts a highlight reel of your life on social media? (Remember when we talked about that in Chapter 1?) Do you feel like you have to project a certain image to the world even if it jars with the truth of your life?

When someone asks you how you are, do you tell them 'fine' or even launch into a list of all the great things that have happened recently when what you really want to say is, 'Things aren't great right now'?

Sometimes, this drive to present a picture-perfect life actually masks a darker truth about feeling trapped.

6.   You are depressed

Many people who feel trapped by something experience depression at some stage, although the symptoms can range from mild to severe.

Depression is very different from feeling sad occasionally. Symptoms include a continuous low mood, feeling hopeless or helpless, feeling tearful, having low self-esteem, feeling guilt-ridden (even without an obvious cause), feeling irritable or intolerant of others, having no motivation or interest in things, finding it difficult to make decisions, feeling anxious or worried, having suicidal thoughts or thoughts about harming yourself, and/or getting no enjoyment out of life.

Depression often comes with a host of physical symptoms too such as changes in weight and appetite, aches and pains, lack of energy, disturbed sleep, moving or speaking more slowly than usual, loss of sex drive and/or brain fog.

If you recognise any of these symptoms and they continue for more than two weeks, it's important to have a chat with your GP.

7.   You use self-harming behaviours such as drinking too much

If you find yourself drinking too much, taking illegal drugs or doing risky things to escape from your current reality, it's a red flag that something in your life needs to change.

8.   You can't say no

Do you struggle to say 'no' to people? Many of us feel like we have to say 'yes' to whatever is asked of us, even if doing so is to our own detriment in some way. People pleasers often feel trapped, running themselves ragged to keep everyone else happy.

Could this be you?

9.   You have low self-esteem

Which came first, low self-esteem or the feeling of being trapped? The two tend to result in a particularly vicious cycle. This is because doing things that don't align with your needs lowers your self-esteem and, in turn, low self-esteem makes you believe that you don't deserve to do what makes you happy, therefore being trapped is inevitable. Each belief feeds the other.

10.   You have commitment issues

Although some people who feel trapped are overly loyal, others struggle to commit. This is because they already feel so trapped by life that they want to exercise control over their relationships by keeping other people at arm's length. Again, this can result in pushing away a potential support system.

Activity Seven: Name your traps

Once again, it's time to grab a few minutes of peace and quiet. Set your phone timer for ten minutes and hit 'Start' when I tell you to.

If someone you trust were to ask you the questions below, what would your answers be?

*   Why can't you do what you want in life?

*   What or whom is stopping you moving forward or being happy living your 'true life'?

*   Why do you feel trapped?

Write down everything that comes to mind. Remember, you don't have to share this list with anyone, and you certainly won't find any judgement from me.

Don't censor yourself – just write down what you can. All I ask is that you're honest with yourself, which I know you will be.

Start!

You can use the space below or print out a worksheet at:

https://www.jobevilacqua.com/resources/

NAME YOUR TRAPS

If someone you trust were to ask you the questions below, what would your answers be?

Why can't you do what you want in life?

_____

_____

_____

_____

_____

What or whom is stopping you from moving forward, being happy and living your "true life"?

_____

_____

_____

_____

_____

Why do you feel trapped?

_____

_____

_____

_____

_____

Obstacles make you stronger

- Unknown

Breaking out of the cage

So, what can you do if you feel trapped? Is it really possible to break out of the cage that you find yourself in?

Absolutely!

I think the first step is recognising why you feel trapped and coming up with achievable steps to make a change.

It may not be easy, but it is 100% possible.

You may be worried about hurting your loved ones and upsetting their lives in order to make yourself happy and I get it, I really do, but this is also a common reason why you become, and stay, trapped – worrying about everyone else's needs before your own.

In most cases, you won't need to burn your entire life to the ground. It's the small, intentional and often gradual changes that can make a huge difference.

So, let's look at this practically. Let's explore the things that you can do to start making the changes needed, step by step actions that you can start implementing to improve your circumstances right now.

If, for example, you feel trapped in life because you're struggling financially, there are steps you can take to improve your circumstances. A quick search on Google for 'budgeting out of debt' or 'get out of debt' will bring up a huge list of resources and links to examples of people who have managed to find financial security after years of debt.

Turn to Pinterest and you can find board after board of advice and resources about budgeting and debt management. I have a couple of boards on my Pinterest profile around this exact subject that I have collected for you to have a look at if you need to. Feel free to follow me on there and I'll follow you back (you can find me at pinterest.co.uk/JoBevilacquaOfficial/).

If you're experiencing financial abuse (or any other abuse), organisations such as Women's Aid (www.womensaid.org.uk) and Refuge (Freephone 24-Hour National Domestic Abuse Helpline: 0808 2000 247) have support services that can help you to come up with a clear plan to change your circumstances.

The same applies to changing careers.

What is it that you really want to do? What do you need to achieve to get there? Could you begin a new course or gain work experience while staying in your current job for the time being?

There are websites such as careershifters.com aimed at people like you who want to change career paths, so why not carve out an hour of your time to have a good look through what help and advice is out there?

Change won't happen overnight, and it could be utterly terrifying, but can you imagine what life might look like from the other side, from the outside of the cage that you feel trapped in?

Give yourself permission to be YOU

One of the most empowering things that you can do is give yourself permission to be you.

If you find that hard, try this ...

Imagine that you're talking to the person you love more than anyone in the world. This might be your child, your romantic partner, a sibling, a parent, a best friend. If they told you they were trapped in some way, what advice would you give them?

You would want them to be happy, wouldn't you?

You would tell them that there is nothing in life that cannot be overcome. You would remind them that they deserve to be loved, to say no, to earn money or to share their talents with the world – whatever it is that would set them free, so tell yourself the same thing.

Activity Eight: Imagine being free of your traps

It's time to let your imagination run wild. If you were completely free of all the things you feel are trapping you, what would your life look like? Imagine all of the challenges and difficult decisions being a thing of the past.

It's time to claim some quiet time and write down everything that you imagine. Try to visualise the details. You might want to include things, feelings, activities, words or phrases – all of the things that will light you up.

If you don't feel comfortable writing things down, you could try creating a dream board or vision board instead – see chapter 7 to find out how.

You can use the space below or print out a worksheet at:

https://www.jobevilacqua.com/resources/

VISUALISE THE LUXURIES

If you were completely free of all the things trapping you, what would your life look like?

1._____

2._____

3._____

4._____

5._____

_____

_____

_____

_____

_____

_____

_____

_____

_____

_____

_____

_____

_____

Claim your power

When you feel trapped, it's easy to blame other people or even the wider world for why you can't break free.

A harsh but necessary truth is that we each have control over our own lives and only you can change something that makes you unhappy. This knowledge can be frightening, especially if you don't yet trust your own instincts or have the confidence to do so but, ultimately, I hope you find the process of reading this book and completing the carefully-selected activities empowering. I hope it helps you towards gaining the confidence and clarity you need.

You have the key to your cage; now is the time to turn it and set yourself free, one step at a time.

You don't have to be trapped at the bottom of the list anymore.

REFLECTION TIME

How do you feel?

_____

_____

_____

What have you learnt?

_____

_____

_____

What will you change?

_____

_____

_____

What will you do more of?

_____

_____

_____

What will you do less of?

_____

_____

_____

Does this raise any strong feelings for you?
(This is your gut telling you that there's a potential issue you need to address)

_____

_____

_____

Do you have any questions?

_____

_____

_____

When you're in a dark place, you sometimes tend to think you've been buried.

Perhaps you've been planted.

Bloom.

- *Unknown*

Chapter 7:

Working out what you want

(Discover who you are, what makes YOU
happy and what you really, really want)

Despite knowing that you need things in your life to change so that you come higher up on your own list, do you struggle to know what it is that you really want?

You're not alone.

For many people, this is the real sticking point.

Not knowing what you want in life can happen for many reasons: low self-esteem, lack of confidence, having always lived according to other people's agendas and expectations, lack of opportunities and fear can all influence you.

Even people who are good all-rounders in life – the straight A students at school – often struggle to pinpoint what it is that they really want. These people can turn their hands to most things, making it harder to identify their greatest talent or potential vocation. You'll often hear these people say (and you might be one of them), 'I still don't know what I want to be when I grow up'.

Depending on your life experiences, you may not know what is available to you in life. Or you may have been taught not to dream too big. There are a million and one reasons why it's hard to know what you want in life, and a million and one people who live their whole lives without any clear purpose.

But is that how you want to live?

Personally, I need to have things to strive for, even though I accept that my plans might change as I grow and evolve over the years. I thrive when I turn my attention to the things that light me up and give meaning to my life.

And I want the same for you, if that is what you want for you too.

Ways to find out what you really want from life

I think there are six key things that you can do to start to unlock what you really want from life, some of which we've already touched on in previous chapters.

1. Listen to your inner voice

Really, this whole book is about the fact that you can never tap into what you want from life if you're always bottom of the list (or not on the list at all). Give yourself permission to listen to your gut when you're presented with decisions and new opportunities. What is it that you want to say before you think of all the reasons that you can't? This inner voice – the one that speaks before you overthink – is the one that will help you to find your direction.

2. Regret nothing

It might be a bit of a cliché, but life really is too short for regrets. I know it's hard but try not to regret the past; every twist and turn has made you the person you are today. And if that person needs work, that's OK – none of us is a finished product yet!

3. Figure out what you need

Do you remember the 'Dare to Dream' activity? You wrote down all of your dreams for the future. This list will help you figure out what you need from life, be it more time with your family, freedom to express yourself, financial security, love, a career change or something else.

4. Name what really bothers you

Sometimes, small changes can set your life on a happier course. For example, you may say that you hate your job, but do you really? Can you be specific about what you hate? Are there parts of your job that you love but other parts that drive you to distraction? If so, is there anything you can do to fix the things that bother you?

As an example, an in-house graphic designer might love the design work they do for a certain type of client but hate the endless meetings, office politics or having to answer to a micro-manager. By going freelance and marketing specifically to the kind of clients they love, they could transform their graphic design career without having to walk away from their love and talent altogether.

5. Acknowledge the things that make you happy

Life can be so busy, so noisy and so downright demanding that it's often easy to miss small moments of happiness. This is especially the case if you've been feeling down about certain aspects of your life for a while.

As you go through your day, I want you to recognise and stop to acknowledge the things that make you happy, no matter how big or small.

Is it the prospect of meeting up with friends, playing with your children, not playing with your children (yeah, I said it), spending time alone with your partner, painting, gardening, exercising, travelling, visiting galleries or museums or catching up on lost sleep…?

The possibilities are endless. What counts is that recognising what makes you happy will help you to build up a picture of the life you want to live.

Try this: A great little exercise is to end every day by writing a list of five things that made you smile or for which you're grateful that day. I love doing this because it switches your brain from what you lack in life to all the special things you have, and you may start seeing a pattern of things that make you happy.

6. Stay positive

Things won't always work out in life. Sometimes roadblocks and unexpected detours will throw themselves in your path, but 'not now' doesn't have to mean 'never'.

When life does throw you a curveball, think about how you feel. Does your goal still matter to you? If it does, try to control what you can and remind yourself that you're just taking a different route to your chosen destination.

Why you need a vision board (and how to create one)

One of the most effective and fun tools I've ever come across for working out what you want in life is a 'vision' board (sometimes called a 'dream' board).

A vision board is a creative process to set clear intentions and goals for what you want in your life, so that you can work towards them and grow and transform yourself. The idea is to create a visual guide to what you want to achieve because it will help you to stay focused on attracting and building the life that you really want.

Above all, it should show your goals as if they've been realised. For example, include a picture of your dream house, your perfect holiday, your ideal dog, your business, dream travel destinations, how much you want to earn or how much money you plan to have in the bank five years from now.

Your vision board should represent all of your key goals, but its format will depend on you and what resonates most deeply.

Vision boards can include a mass of different subjects such as wealth, health, fitness, material things, feelings, family, friends, work, business, personal development, home, fun, experiences and/or quotes.

Some people use large boards over which they pin or glue photos, quotes, newspaper and magazine cuttings, postcards, ticket stubs, wrapping paper, stickers, etc. Anything that reflects their aspirations. Other people use bullet journals, Canva, Word, PowerPoint, a design program or Pinterest to express their vision for the future.

At the vision boarding workshops I run, we always encourage making a physical 'vision' board. In fact, we take over the room with big A3 pieces of card, magazines, scissors and glue – it's so much fun!

I always recommend laying out everything you want to include and then playing with different arrangements to see what captures your attention and fits you best.

Write the date on the back so that you can reflect back on your vision. You can create vision boards at any time for individual goals, at the start of a new year, a new chapter in your life or the launch of a new business service. It's really up to you. There is no right or wrong.

Personally, I have one board that I redo every couple of years, made up of both big and small goals. This means that there are some quick wins that give me a boost as well as the confidence to keep working towards and achieving the bigger goals on there too.

Once your vision board is complete, make sure you display it somewhere you'll regularly see it. This could be over your desk, by your front door, in your bedroom or even as a photograph on your phone's screensaver.

It's essential that you see your vision board as often as possible so that your brain starts adopting the potential outcomes of your goals as a reality.

Your life doesn't get better by chance. It gets better by change.

- Jim Rohn

Activity Nine: Your vision board

You can use the space over the page to create your vision board. Think about what you want your life to look like five, ten or even twenty years from now.

Who are you? What would you achieve if there was nothing and no-one holding you back? What are the things your heart desires? What words, phrases or visuals on your board stand out to you?

I want you to spend at least an hour on this. Ideally, I'd love you to do this when you've got some alone time, but I know that might not be possible. If you've got kids at home, maybe you could get them to do some cutting and sticking on their own boards to give you the time and space to be creative.

If you really want to invest some time and space to do this, then it might be worth searching online for vision boarding workshops. There may be one planned near you and if not, why not check out the ones I host and come and join me and others in my community in person? How great would that be?!

My vision board

My vision board

Decide what kind of life you really want… and then say no to everything that isn't that.

- *Unknown*

REFLECTION TIME

How do you feel?

_____

_____

_____

What have you learnt?

_____

_____

_____

What will you change?

_____

_____

_____

What will you do more of?

_____

_____

_____

What will you do less of?

_____

_____

_____

Does this raise any strong feelings for you?
(This is your gut telling you that there's a potential issue you need to address)

_____

_____

_____

Do you have any questions?

_____

_____

_____

Chapter 8:

Dealing with other people's expectations

(Figuring out where pressures come from in life and how to escape them)

How to be a parent in 2017

Make sure your children's academic, emotional, psychological, mental, spritual, physical, nutritional and social needs are met while being careful not to over stimulate, under stimulate, improperly medicate, helicopter or neglect them in a screen-free, processed food free, GMO free, negitive energy-free, plastic-free, body positive, socially consious, egalitarian but also authoritative, nuturing but fostering of independence, gentle but not overly permissive, pesticide free, multilingual home, preferably in a cul-de-sac with a backyard and 1.5 siblings spaced at least two years apart. Also, don't forget the cocnut oil.

How to be a parent in literally every generation before ours:

Feed them sometimes.

(This is why we're crazy).

Bunmi Laditan

Many women tell me that no matter what they do and how hard they try they never feel that they're doing a good enough job. The pressure and the expectation to do everything and be there for everyone feels relentless.

This absolutely breaks my heart, not only because I can identify with how emotionally draining it all is but because of how unfair it is too. To add to that, I just don't see it getting any better in the future unless we acknowledge what's happening and make conscious, intentional decisions to not accept it anymore.

We need to do this both individually and collectively.

The first time I saw Bunmi Laditan's quote above, it actually made me laugh out loud. Not only did I find it funny, I also found it very, very sad. Every single word hit me harder than that last.

In just 125 words this quote manages to sum up the pressure and expectations on women – especially mums – in our society today. Honestly, I believe that this pressure is one of the most significant contributing factors to why women everywhere are riddled with mum guilt and feeling like they're never 'enough'.

Whenever I talk to my female friends, no matter what their situation or their choices, there's a unanimous feeling that they should be doing things differently, which is really code for 'better'.

Where does this pressure come from?

All the conversations got me thinking: when do we first start taking on other people's expectations and try to live up to them?

For most of us, external pressure and expectations become evident from an early age. They come from our immediate families, our wider circles, society, our teachers and our peers. Eventually, we internalise the pressure so that it's coming at us from inside as well as outside.

Of course, pressure and expectation aren't exclusive to women. Men experience them too. However, it's women that we're interested in here because this book is all about helping you – the women I see and hear so clearly – to break free from the very real pressures you face as a woman. The pressures that result in you always putting yourself last on the list.

More opportunities = more opportunities to be judged!

We're told daily that women have more opportunities and choices than ever before. While this is great for lots of reasons, it also gives so many more opportunities for people to judge.

Isn't it amazing how many people think it's OK to share their opinions on what they think is the right or wrong way to live, even when their opinion isn't asked for?! Grrrrrr!

These opinions cover the lot: the subjects we women choose to study at school; if we go to uni or not; what career we choose; the friends we keep; the partner we choose; what we wear; how we spend our money; when/ if we get married; when/if we have children; if we have a 'natural' birth or a C-section; if we breastfeed or bottle feed; if we co-sleep or sleep train our children; if we go back to work or not post-kids; if fitness is our priority or not; our weight; our size; what we eat; our age; our temperament; and so on …

No wonder that when you ask another woman how she's doing, more often than not she'll respond with how tired she is, it's exhausting.

Sound familiar?

You may feel that you have been judged in one or many of the above situations. Or, when consciously thinking about it, you may have even formed and shared your own opinions on other people's situations or choices.

I think we're all guilty of that at some point in our lives, aren't we?

I mean, we're all encouraged to share our opinions every day and we're fascinated with other people's opinions, so much so that there are magazines and TV shows centred solely on people giving their opinions.

We even make judgements subconsciously without being aware of it. These judgements often come from biases that we've picked up from our families, our wider culture and society, our peer groups and our experiences.

In workplaces, for example, people often demonstrate types of unconscious bias such as an employer wanting to hire someone that went to the same university as them or because they share a similar background or not wanting to hire someone because of their ethnicity, gender, socio-economic background or age.

While this bias may not be conscious, it can be destructive.

Everything we learn in life can influence what we expect of people, both positively and negatively. That works both ways, informing what other people expect of us too.

Our careers and/or motherhood vs. other people's opinions

In my experience, the two biggest areas in a woman's life that bring forward unasked for opinions and judgements are her role as a mother and her career, especially when the two overlap.

A woman can be a stay at home mum, part-time working mum, full-time employed mum, mum who owns her own business or not a mum at all, BUT what all these have in common is the feeling that we should be doing things differently or, as I said earlier, 'better'.

Worse still, there's the sense of being judged by those around us which often weighs heavily on our shoulders. It can seem like no matter what we do it's a weight we'll never shift.

What's the saying? 'Damned if you do, damned if you don't.'

For example, many stay at home mums feel like they're putting additional pressure on their partners to support the family financially while they stay at home with their children. Then, because they chose to stay at home, they feel like they're supposed to enjoy every single minute, forfeiting the right to moan about their situation no matter how difficult the day or the children may have been for them.

Meanwhile, the full-time working mums feel guilty for leaving the office at 5 p.m. on the dot to make the nursery pick up. They worry that their colleagues doubt their commitment every time they have to take a day off to look after a poorly little one. They feel guilty for missing time with their children because of work. They wonder if their children will suffer in some way for the daily time apart.

Name any situation and I bet I can name countless expectations that will make women feel guilty!

The external pressure from other people's opinions can cause a kind of paralysis in us, where we struggle to make decisions for fear of making the wrong choices or letting other people down. Sometimes, you can have heard other people's opinions for so long that it becomes hard to separate out what you want for yourself versus what other people expect of you.

How do you deal with other people's opinions?

You may be the type of person to brush off other people's opinions quite easily but, more likely, their comments over the years will have stuck with you. You may even have altered what you do and why you do it to please other people and to fit in.

Having your decisions and choices questioned and challenged can have a massive knock-on effect on your self-esteem. In turn, this results in you having less confidence in yourself and the choices you make, making you far more likely to become stuck – stuck, uninspired and scared to do anything that could lead to more criticism from the people around you.

I understand because I've felt this way too, way more than I would ever have wanted.

In this mindset, it's easy to start relying on external sources in society more and more to tell you what's expected of you. You can find yourself buying all the books, watching all the programmes, reading all the magazines, watching all the influencers, etc., all in the hope of finding someone who will tell you the 'right' way to live, the way to earn you other people's approval.

But the truth is that there is no 'right' way to live. Someone will always have an opinion about how you live your life. But their focus on you simply reflects their own story, their own experiences and their own self-esteem – they play it out in words or looks, opinions and judgements.

The way I look at it, if someone is adamant that you should do things a certain way, regardless of your feelings, it will either come from their lack of understanding, their insecurities, their low self-esteem or their need for control.

If someone is truly happy in their own life and wants the best for you, why would they feel the need to put pressure on you to do, say or feel anything apart from what you truly want?

Letting go of other people's expectations

The reality is that there will always be expectations and pressure. What matters is that you don't have to bend your life to them.

As we've seen, there will always be someone to disapprove of our choices, regardless of what those choices are. Knowing this, surely the only way to move forward is to make the choices that are best for us and our loved ones?

Right?

If other people disapprove of our choices, that's for them to come to terms with, not us. Of course, letting go of other people's expectations doesn't usually happen overnight. Often, when we've been bending over backwards to please everyone else, we end up losing sight of what would truly make us feel happy and fulfilled.

If you've always shaped your life around other people's opinions and input, whether that's from your parents, a partner, your children, teachers, colleagues, bosses or friends, pinpointing what you want, what you feel and what you believe can be surprisingly hard.

But it is possible, I assure you.

Below are a few tips to help you let go of other people's expectations and start creating realistic, fair expectations of yourself, for yourself.

Steps you can take to create realistic expectations

1. Practice self-care

Self-care is about more than having a bubble bath or reading for pleasure at the end of a long day.

In reality, it's about facing up to your life and putting a plan in action to change or nurture the things that affect your wellbeing, be it creating more positives or eliminating more negatives. It's about finding a way out of debt, cooking nutritious meals or spending time with people who treat you well. It's about creating a life that you don't regularly want or need to escape from.

And one of the first ways to practice self-care is to let go of other people's expectations. You may have to disappoint people and you may have to say no, but that's OK. Saying no doesn't make you a bad person.

2. Speak to yourself with the kindness you would show a friend

When you're struggling with the weight of other people's expectations, your thoughts can become bogged down with ideas about what you 'should' and 'must' do, as well as what you 'can't' achieve (remember those limiting beliefs we talked about in Chapter 5?). This means the voice inside your head can become mean and critical, a running commentary of your failings or your fears.

Would you speak to your best friend the way you speak to yourself? Or to your child?

I imagine that if someone spoke to one of your children the way you talk to yourself internally, you'd be horrified. It would bring out the protective mama lion in you.

Well, this is the time to parent yourself with kindness, to speak to yourself with the compassion and understanding you would give a best friend.

I read once that self-compassion is like fresh oxygen for the mind. It releases oxytocin, the 'happy' hormone, and lifts your mood. Give it a try.

3. Recognise that other people's expectations aren't really about you

When one person sets expectations of another person, it's often because they assume everyone thinks the same way as them or because they need validation and approval about their own decisions.

For example, if someone has told you, as a business owner, that you should 'go out and get a proper job', it might be because they want to reinforce that they were right to stay in their own job, even if it didn't fulfil them in the same way as being self-employed fulfils you.

Expectations can also be about control.

It might be a case of you staying in your lane and doing everything for everyone else so other people can continue to do what they want. They can achieve particular outcomes because of that.

Control can also come from a place where the other person feels that your decisions reflect on them. This was something that I experienced as a teen and young adult. I know that there was an expectation from my dad that I would do well at school, get my A-levels and go to university and, as long as I did, he would financially support me.

Education was very important to him and it was something that I always felt was a non-negotiable for him. So, even though I didn't want to, I enrolled into sixth form after my GCSEs to please him but subsequently dropped out. The same then happened when I signed up to a Business Studies course at college the next September. I left half-way through to work full-time in what would turn out to be my favourite and most educating job, selling mobile phones at Phones 4 U. I loved the buzz I got from making money through helping people, a feeling that has never left me.

But it's safe to say that although I was doing what made me happy, concentrating on getting real-life work experience, my dad was less than happy with my choices. I believe he felt it reflected badly on him at the time and it caused a bit of a disconnection between us for a couple of years. Luckily, being true to myself and time has resulted in us now being closer than ever.

What I'm trying to share here is that you don't have to want the same outcomes as other people. You are not a tool to be used for someone else's gain or to reinforce how they want to be seen in the world. That's their responsibility. Yours is to control where your life is going.

4. Trust your gut

When you do or say anything, take a moment to consider how it feels on an instinctive or 'gut' level. Does it feel right, good and truthful to who you are, or does it feel uncomfortable?

If something feels off (often with physical symptoms such as a churning stomach or faster heart rate), it probably isn't right for you and may well reflect someone else's expectations rather than your own intentions.

Take the time to learn how your body reacts when faced with certain situations and learn the difference between the emotions and what could be red flags.

5. Be open to what you could achieve

If you haven't gathered already, other people's expectations can hold us back in so many ways.

For example, you may have been brought up with a 'scarcity' or 'lack of' mentality around money. You may have heard things like 'money doesn't grow on trees' or you may have had to go without things that your friends had. You may even have heard your parents arguing about money or them being verbally worried about not being able to pay the bills.

Situations like this can cause you to consciously or subconsciously believe that you're destined to just get by and that there will never be enough money to do what you really want to do in life, even as an adult.

With this expectation drilled into you before you were old enough to question it, you may avoid investing in yourself or your business. You may feel you have to stay in an unhappy relationship or an unfulfilling job because you'll never earn enough to take a different path, that you should be happy with 'your lot' and that you're ungrateful for wanting anything more.

But what if you started looking at things in a different way?

What if you decided that you could achieve more with a plan in place to help you? And then what if you went about creating and sticking to the plan? It really is as simple as that. We just complicate it by hanging on to our limiting beliefs and putting every else's needs ahead of our own.

Small changes can make a big difference. Recognise that you have potential to do, be and earn whatever you want and do whatever makes you happy.

6. Set boundaries and restate them when you need to

When we build our lives around other's expectations, we often haven't put any boundaries in place. People are able to voice their opinions without being asked or drop things on you at the last minute with no consideration of how that might impact on you because they've never been told otherwise.

Practice naming your limits. This can be challenging if you're not used to setting boundaries, but you are allowed – and, in fact, I encourage you – to state what you will tolerate and accept, as well as what you won't.

If you feel uncomfortable or resentful about something, it's a big clue that a boundary has been breached. Give yourself permission to say no. You may need to restate your boundaries from time to time and when you do, stick by them, regardless of what reaction you get from others.

7. Set realistic goals

The myth of perfection means that we end up thinking that we should always be happy, fulfilled and busy doing something worthwhile, living Instagram-ready moments every waking minute of the day.

We feel like our life should be full of big defining moments and accomplishments.

Striving for perfection means we need to be the best mum, run the best business or even just make the biggest splash at a networking event. It's all about comparing yourself to others and coming out on top.

Life becomes a tick list of accomplishments above anything else.

We've been conditioned to believe that to live the 'perfect life' we have to do well at school, go to university, meet someone, get married, buy a house, have two children, get rich, travel the world, retire at 50, blah blah blah. All of these big 'life markers' are what we are supposed to be aspiring to, apparently, with no blueprint for how to do these things or even any consideration about if they're right for us.

Reality is, well, more real than that, and perhaps a little more mundane. It's made up of small moments, the things that happen, good and bad, while we're busy making plans.

So, instead of the huge goals, letting go of other people's expectations lets you set smaller, more realistic goals based on what's right for you.

Instead of thinking happiness is waiting somewhere in the future when you've ticked off every item on the list, you can start to find happiness in the here and now.

8. Celebrate your victories

As I mentioned previously, expectations set you up to seek perfection. Even when you achieve something, other people's expectations can overshadow your accomplishments. Instead, you're always looking around the corner for the next thing you need to tick off your to-do list.

Try to take time to celebrate your victories, big and small.

You don't have to hold a party (unless you want to) or declare a national holiday but give yourself a moment to acknowledge every achievement. That way you can begin to see yourself as someone who gets things done, who makes things happen and who is capable.

Why not go one step further and keep a diary, a journal or a scrapbook of successes? Or you could share your achievements on your social media or write a blog about them. One thing I've realised is that sharing successes not only reminds you of the good stuff that has happened or what you are capable of, but it also gives others permission to share their successes too.

9. Own your choices

When you live your life based on other people's expectations, it's easy to feel like life is something that's happening to you rather than something you have a say in shaping. Like a rudderless boat, you feel you're powerless against the tide. But this can leave you feeling like an incidental character in your own life story.

When you own your choices in life, you can begin to let go of other people's expectations. You stop being someone things happen to and become the hero with flaws and unique superpowers. And, I mean, who doesn't want to be a superhero, even if it's just in our own life?!

Start small and work up

As with any new skill, letting go of expectations takes practice. It's like a muscle that you need to exercise and strengthen before it feels easy to use it. So, give yourself permission to start small if you need to.

Acknowledge that there is pressure in our current society to fit a template but that sometimes the best works of art are those that break the mould. What's the saying? 'Well behaved women seldom make history.'

Challenge your thoughts and pay attention to your feelings. I bet you'll find that your body knows what you need, even if you think your mind doesn't.

Make a list of the pressures in your life and then think about how you could relieve them.

Ask for help if you need to.

Remember that 'no' is a complete sentence – you don't have to justify your reply if something doesn't work for you.

Just because you are right doesn't mean that I am wrong.

You just haven't seen life from my side.

- Unknown

REFLECTION TIME

How do you feel?

_____

_____

_____

What have you learnt?

_____

_____

_____

What will you change?

_____

_____

_____

What will you do more of?

_____

_____

_____

What will you do less of?

_____

_____

_____

Does this raise any strong feelings for you?
(This is your gut telling you that there's a potential issue you need to address)

_____

_____

_____

Do you have any questions?

_____

_____

_____

Chapter 9:

Stop making excuses!

(Discover what's really stopping you & imagine how you
could soar if you broke through your blocks)

Do you often find yourself making excuses, especially for why you can't, shouldn't, couldn't or didn't do something?

When things go badly or you make a mistake, are you quick to come up with a list of 'reasons' to explain what happened?

Do you make excuses when things don't go your way or come up with explanations to justify your procrastination?

In truth, we all make excuses from time to time. Excuses are a way to rationalise why we aren't able to go through with a specific commitment. We talked about this a little in the limiting beliefs chapter, didn't we?

Where excuses become a problem is when you make them all the time.

What excuses are holding you back?

'Excuses are the nails used to build a house of failure.' – Don Wilder

We can always find a reason not to pursue our dreams, not to take action or not to upset the status quo. The 'reasons' we give often seem perfectly… well… reasonable.

With a well-practised list of excuses, it's incredibly easy to justify why you can't do something in life.

Common excuses include phrases like:

* I don't have enough time

* It's too late/hard/complicated

* I'm too young/old/tired/busy

* I can't afford it

* I'm waiting for inspiration to strike

* It will take too long

* I'll start tomorrow/next week/next month/next year

* If it was meant to be, it would have happened by now

* It's not possible with my other commitments

* I can't neglect the people who need me/I can't let anyone down

* I'm not clever/talented/experienced enough

* I'm not sure it's the right thing

* I don't know how to do that

* I need to wait until the kids are older/it doesn't fit with our family life

* I don't have any support or the right connections

* The economy is too unpredictable at the moment

* I can't beat the competition

* I don't have the right skills

* I don't know where to start

* Too many people have tried and failed – why should I be different?

Do any of these excuses sound familiar?

Activity Ten: Recognise your excuses

Sometimes excuses sound so reasonable that you might not even recognise that you're making them.

For this exercise, I want you to take ten minutes to think about the biggest dream you've identified so far in this book (what featured most prominently on your vision board in Chapter 7?) and then jot down all the reasons why your dream isn't possible right now.

You can use the space over the page or print out a worksheet at:

https://www.jobevilacqua.com/resources/

RECOGNISE YOUR EXCUSES

Take ten minutes to think about the biggest dream you've identified so far in this book and then jot down all the reasons why you believe that your dream isn't possible right now
(leave a line between each one).

My dream is not possible because...

_____

_____

_____

_____

_____

_____

_____

_____

_____

_____

_____

_____

_____

_____

_____

It's time to start making changes

If there's a goal in your life that you keep making excuses about, could it be that you don't want it as much as you think you do? This is often a clue that the goal you're chasing comes from other people's expectations rather than what you truly want for yourself.

If there's reluctance behind your excuses, then now is the time to give yourself permission to forget a goal that no longer serves you.

Honestly, forget about it!

Remember, the magic in life happens where you place your attention. From now on, I only want you to focus on the things that really light you up inside.

If the goal in your life is genuinely yours though and your excuses are simply born out of fear, please don't beat yourself up about it. We all feel frightened sometimes, myself included. The first step to making changes is to stop being hard on yourself and to get out of your own wretched way.

Excuses are a form of self-sabotage; once you recognise them for what they are, they start to lose their power. Let me ask you, if you put your excuses to one side and started working towards your goals, what's the worst that could happen? OK, you might fail and end up where you are now, but you'll be stuck here anyway, even if you do nothing.

So, let's spin that fear on its head and have a look at life from the other side of your worries. What if you succeed? What if you reach your goal? How amazing would that feel? What would that look like?

It's a good thought, isn't it?

The real reasons behind excuses — and how to break through them!

After doing some research, there are apparently 10 broad 'truths' behind the excuses we make in life. Below, we're going to take a closer look at what these truths are and how you can break through the blocks that are holding you back:

Truth #1: You're frightened

It's natural to feel frightened about the unknown. On the most primitive level it's our brains keeping us safe from potential threats, but in the modern world fear isn't about avoiding wolves and bears, instead it can just keep us locked in our comfort zones. While our comfort zones are comfortable by definition, if you can't move out of them, they're nothing more than a prison.

Knowledge and familiarity are the antidotes to fear. Your brain is frightened because it doesn't know what to expect, so the best way to overcome fear-based excuses is to arm yourself with as much information as possible.

Somewhere in the world, someone else will have achieved the things you want to achieve (or something like them). What's their story? What did they do? How did they get from where you are now to where they wanted to be?

If you can find out how somebody achieved what you want to achieve, it will help to break down your fear. It's the psychological equivalent of climbing a cliff face – if someone can give you the right equipment and route through the rocks, suddenly the climb doesn't seem as daunting as it would if you went rogue.

Truth #2: You don't want to fail

Do you have a strong perfectionist streak? Were you raised to believe that you shouldn't ever make mistakes? Or that nine out of ten wasn't good enough?

This kind of thinking holds so many people back in life. We end up believing that we have to do something brilliantly on the first attempt or otherwise we shouldn't bother trying. This can result in you doing nothing new, ever.

Fear of failure means we end up standing still, not putting ourselves out there in case it goes wrong.

The reality is that it's OK to fail. In fact, it's more than OK. We're human; we all do it. And, in my experience, our failures in life are often where the biggest, most important lessons are to be found.

A child doesn't get up and walk the first time they try. They fall over hundreds of times before they take their first step and every time they fall, they learn a bit more about what they need to do to succeed. It doesn't make them any less of a walker when they've cracked it, does it?

Give yourself permission to fail and recognise failure as a chance to learn something new.

Truth #3: You're scared of making mistakes

Like Truth #2 above, many of us are terrified of making mistakes in life. Mistakes are embarrassing, aren't they? They make us vulnerable or announce our 'weaknesses' to the world. We worry that people will think less of us if we do something wrong.

But, in common with failure, mistakes usually provide the best learning opportunities. If we can pinpoint where we've gone wrong with something, we can learn how to do it better in the future.

Think about some of the greatest artists, designers, inventors and creators in the world. I imagine their creations were built on a foundation of prototypes, experiments and mistakes.

If the thought of making a mistake brings you out in a rash, the best way to banish your excuses is to proactively learn about a task first, either by watching tutorials, talking to a mentor, taking classes or learning in the privacy of your own home. The more prepared you are, the less likely you'll be to make mistakes. But if they do happen, look at what you can learn.

Truth #4: You don't know what to expect

Uncertainty is unsettling. When you make changes in your life, the uncertainty comes from having no previous experience or perspective on which to base your expectations of the future. In this situation, it's really easy to make assumptions or jump to conclusions about what might happen. Many of us live out whole future scenarios in our minds, which is often a sign of anxiety.

An incredibly powerful way of dealing with uncertainty is an approach known as 'If-then planning'. This is when you plan for potential future outcomes by saying, 'If <insert a potential obstacle> happens, then I will do <insert action/response>'.

Let me give you an example. Imagine I want to study a business qualification at university but I'm worried that I can't afford it, don't have the right qualifications and that my kids are too young. My if-then planning could look something like this:

* **If** I speak to the admissions office and they confirm that I don't have the right qualifications to apply, **then** I will find out what entry qualifications I need and contact local FE colleges to see if they offer them.

* **If** I can't afford the course fees, **then** I will contact the university's student finance office to find out what funding might be available.

* **If** the university doesn't have a nursery, **then** I will ask my friends and family if they know of a reliable local childminder.

* **If** a full-time degree isn't possible, **then** I will find out if I can apply to do it part-time.

If you have a strategy for how to handle obstacles, it will be much tougher to make excuses about not carrying on.

Truth #5: You don't have a specific goal

If you're not exactly sure what it is that you want to achieve or your goal is just so far away that it's not relatable, then it's far easier to make excuses.

One common non-specific goal is 'I want to lose weight' but it's so vague that it's completely open to abuse! You can end up telling yourself, 'I've lost a pound so I deserve a piece of cake, and a Chinese takeaway, and a glass of wine'.

Instead, try setting goals that are specific, measurable, attainable, realistic and time-bound (so-called SMART goals). Using the above example, a SMART goal would be something like, 'I plan to lose 10lbs over the next six weeks by reducing my calorie intake to XXXX calories a day and exercising for 30 minutes three times a week'.

This goal gives you a plan for what you want to achieve and how you're going to achieve it. It's much harder to make excuses when you know exactly what you need to do.

Want to know more about SMART goals? We'll be talking about them in Chapter 17.

Truth #6: You compare yourself to others

In this book we've already talked a fair bit about feeling like you don't measure up to other people or that everyone is in on the secret to living life successfully. One of the most common comparisons I see is from self-employed mums who assume that other female entrepreneurs are miles ahead of them in their businesses.

As the saying goes, it's like comparing apples to oranges. Everyone has different starting points, different circumstances or different commitments so we can never fairly compare ourselves to someone else. This is the same inside and outside of the business world.

If you focus on what everyone else is doing, you'll never give yourself a chance to discover what you're great at.

Remember, you're unique. When you look at others, you're seeing the result and not the effort. Who knows what struggles the other person is having or has had behind the scenes?

Above all, comparison kills the joy of achievement. I want you to celebrate your successes in your own right.

Truth #7: You don't feel motivated

Change is hard work! If you often find excuses, it could be because you don't feel motivated enough to make a change.

Again, it's worth asking if what you're working towards is really your own goal. Perhaps you think you should want something because it's what other people have said you should want.

If you don't feel motivated right now, what would step your motivation up a gear? How can you raise the stakes to make you more invested in succeeding?

Truth #8: You lack the resources

As we saw earlier in this chapter, some of the most common excuses in life revolve around a lack of resources, be it time, money, skills or education.

In my experience, while you may not have the resources right now, if you want something badly enough in life, the resources can always be found. It can just take some time.

If, for example, you're struggling financially, your immediate goals might be around cutting out unnecessary spending, selling some of your belongings, taking on a side hustle to earn more money or seeking debt management support.

Once you're on top of your immediate resource issues, you can extend your goals to your longer-term aspirations, such as using the money you've saved to launch a business or pay for your continuing education.

Truth #9: You're set in your ways

This is always an uncomfortable truth to admit but the reality is that many of us make excuses in life because we get set in our ways. It's that thing of 'I am who I am' or 'This is how I've always done things' but – the saying goes – 'If you do what you've always done, you'll get what you've always got'.

If you want things to change in your life the first thing you may need to change is you or, more specifically, your outlook. It may take time and be completely alien, but it will be worth every small evolution.

Truth #10: You're protecting yourself

Change is scary. What if your goals are wrong? What if you get hurt? What if you walk away or adapt something so much that you can never come back to what you know now?

These are natural thoughts but, on the other hand, what if it all works out? How amazing would that be?

Often, we make excuses because our brains are protecting us from the great unknown.

Our sense of self is so important that it could be you're scared of losing your identity while you're making changes. This is something I hear a lot from women I work with. They feel that by concentrating on their career development somehow their identity as a mother might become compromised.

In my experience, change will happen even if we don't plan for it. I bet you're a very different person today to the person you were 20 years ago. Change is a good thing, especially if you're in control of it. So, let's embrace it!

The thing about excuses

Along with limiting beliefs, excuses are often about self-protection, but the truth is that they're holding you back from realising your true potential. Excuses can damage your career, your relationships, your health and wellbeing and so much more.

I also believe that excuses lead you down a path of regrets as you look back on 'the road not taken' in life and long for all the opportunities that slipped through your fingers.

That path isn't for someone as fantastic as you. YES, YOU!

From today, I really encourage you to:

* Stop comparing yourself to others

* Stop fearing the unknown – instead of thinking about what could go wrong, focus on what could go right!

* Stop blaming others

* Take responsibility for ALL of your actions

* Take action every day, even if it's something small

* Set small, attainable goals

* Learn from your mistakes

* Focus on your strengths

*   Embrace your power to change

*   Visualise your success

*   Give yourself permission to be imperfect

*   Believe in yourself

Don't 'fake it 'til you make it'. That's garbage advice.

Face it 'til you make it.

Get up. Work hard. Fail. Stand back up. Face it again. Do a little better. Fail again. Get back up.

Repeat.

- Jordan Syatt

REFLECTION TIME

How do you feel?

_____

_____

_____

What have you learnt?

_____

_____

_____

What will you change?

_____

_____

_____

What will you do more of?

_____

_____

_____

What will you do less of?

_____

_____

_____

Does this raise any strong feelings for you?
(This is your gut telling you that there's a potential issue you need to address)

_____

_____

_____

Do you have any questions?

_____

_____

_____

Chapter 10:

Relationships

(Recognising which are working for you & which aren't)

The relationships you have in your life – with your romantic partners, family, friends and colleagues – will affect where you appear on your own list of priorities.

If you're involved in plenty of healthy relationships they will empower and strengthen you. On the flip side, just one or two unhealthy relationships in your life can really start to chip away at your self-esteem.

When you think of the most important relationships in your life right now, how do you feel about them? Do the people around you make you feel loved and supported? A big 'yay' to all those that do. I genuinely am so pleased for you.

Maybe there are some relationships that need a bit of work or, if you're honest, actually make you feel pretty miserable? The latter breaks my heart.

In this chapter, I want us to take a look together at why it's so important to nurture your healthy relationships and why it's OK to walk away from relationships that no longer work for you.

What makes a healthy relationship?

A healthy relationship allows both parties to feel supported and connected at the same time as feeling independent. Communication and boundaries are two major components. Above all, a healthy relationship is one that enriches your life, bringing you more happiness than it does stress.

Healthy relationships take work to maintain, whether we're talking about work relationships, friendships, family relationships or romantic relationships.

The common ground is that any healthy, positive relationship in your life should be built on:

* Trust

* Honesty

* Respect

* Equality

* Kindness

* Fun

* Independence

It's also important that relationships move at a comfortable pace for both of you (and yes, this includes platonic relationships, not just romantic ones!) and that you can each take responsibility for your words and actions and how they might make the other person feel.

Another sign of a truly healthy relationship is that you can have conflict – perhaps a difference of opinion – and feel safe to express it while knowing that the relationship will survive a disagreement.

What are the signs of unhealthy relationships?

There are many signs of an unhealthy relationship, most of which indicate some sort of inequality between the two people involved.

You may feel like you can't express your opinion without the other person lashing out in some way. You may find yourself being blamed for problems in the relationship or having to account for your every move. You may have no privacy or be pressured into doing things that make you uncomfortable.

If you're always being told by someone close to you that you're 'too sensitive', 'overreacting' or 'too needy', these can all be red flags that the relationship isn't equal. Be wary of someone who makes you feel like you're not capable of achieving things for yourself or makes you feel like you are always in the wrong - this can be a form of control and a way to chip away at your confidence.

Often, in unhealthy relationships, one person is routinely given priority over the other, meaning that the seemingly 'less important' person's needs are overlooked and neglected. These relationships often influence where you put yourself on your list of priorities. If you're always bottom of your own list, or not on it at all, it could be a sign that there's at least one relationship in your life that needs a healthier balance.

I'm not saying that the relationship has to end. All good relationships take work and it's easy to fall into unhealthy patterns. Better communication and a willingness to meet in the middle can positively transform all kinds of relationships.

On the other hand, sometimes relationships are so damaged, damaging or unequal that the healthiest thing you can do is walk away.

This chapter will hopefully help you establish where your relationships sit, which ones need work and which ones you may need to walk (run) away from.

Activity Eleven: List your current relationships

It's time to grab another ten minutes of peace and quiet. Set the timer on your phone to help keep you focused.

I would like you to make a list of all the relationships that currently shape your life. As well as your partner (if you have one) and kids (if you have any), I want you to list your parents, siblings, friends, other relatives, work relationships, people in your business network, online relationships and so on. Anyone that you would say is part of your current life in some meaningful way.

Ready…steady…hit that timer and GO! You can use the space over the page or print out a worksheet at:

https://www.jobevilacqua.com/resources/

CURRENT RELATIONSHIPS

1._____

2._____

3._____

4._____

5._____

6._____

7._____

8._____

9._____

10._____

11._____

12._____

Avoiding certain people to protect your emotional health is not a weakness.

It's wisdom.

- Unknown

How do you feel about your current relationships?

When you look at the list you've just written, do any relationships leap out at you either because of how good they make you feel or because of how stressful they are?

Do any of these relationships feel unbalanced? Are you the one who puts in all the effort or who always gives way to avoid 'making a fuss'?

Are you surrounded by the right kind of people? In other words, people who don't add pressure, guilt or stress to your life but instead ease the pressure and make you feel heard and supported?

There may be relationships on your list that you would just like to improve in some way, or you may need to start seeking healthy relationships and support from new people and that's ok too.

It's time to set some boundaries

All healthy relationships have boundaries.

If you have any relationships in your life where you feel constantly put upon or like your wishes aren't respected, it's time to re-establish the boundaries – or maybe establish them for the first time!

What does boundary pushing look like?

Here are a few examples that might resonate with your own life.

Imagine you work from home as a freelancer. Despite telling your friends and family that you will be working every day between 9 a.m. and 3 p.m. while the kids are at school, one friend in particular frequently shows up at your door during the day, assuming she can pop in for a cuppa. If you let her in, she often stays for hours at a time, even when you repeatedly tell her that you have work you need to get on with.

Or maybe you have a family member who texts you throughout the day and then feels cross with you if you don't reply immediately.

Or perhaps one of the mums from your child's school always asks you for childcare help – often on short notice – but never offers to return the favour.

These are just a few of the ways in which boundaries can be pushed, overstepped or ignored in our relationships, it may be a good idea for you to acknowledge which one of your boundaries are being pushed and by whom and how you move forward with each of the people listed.

Are you going to spend more time with them becuase they lift you up, less time with those that bring you down, or are there people who need new boundaries and you just need some guidence on how to enforce them?

Walls keep everybody out. Boundaries teach people where the door is.

- Mark Groves

Boundaries need you to actively enforce them

The thing about boundaries in relationships is that they can only be pushed, overstepped or ignored if you allow them to be. And this can be a really tough thing to recognise.

If, using the example above, you always invite your friend in when they come round unannounced for a cuppa, then you're allowing them to disregard your time.

Equally, if a client or boss always drops 'urgent' work on you on a Friday late afternoon/evening, expecting it back for Monday, and you don't say anything about it being the weekend, it's understandable that the client might repeat the same behaviour in the future.

This is where you have to make your boundaries clear, whatever they may be.

You could tell your frequently visiting friend, 'I have a meeting now. Give me a call before you come over next time and then I can make sure I'm in and you won't have a wasted trip'.

Or you could tell your weekend-trashing client that, 'The office closes at 5 p.m. on Friday so I will have to pick this up on Monday morning. The earliest I can get it back to you is by close of play on Tuesday. If it really has to be done over the weekend, I could see about fitting it in but would need to charge a rush fee in addition to the usual price to reflect that it's being done at short notice and over the weekend'. In this scenario it might make the client decide that the work isn't so urgent after all!

As you can see, in most cases you won't need to spell out, 'Hey, I'm setting a boundary here' but that is exactly what you are doing.

Instead, it's usually enough to state what you need and what the consequences might be if the other person ignores you, for example, it will be a wasted journey for them, the work won't get done/will cost more, you won't be available.

To avoid confusion, keep things simple.

You don't have to offer lengthy explanations about your availability/reasons/circumstances. You have every right to look after your own needs.

And remember, 'No' is a complete sentence! You don't have to justify why you don't want to do something. You're not seeking the approval from anyone else anymore, remember?

One final point about boundaries is that they don't have to be set in stone. Right now, you might feel like you're not up to daily phone calls from your mum but at another time in your life you might love that regular contact. The thing with boundaries is that they're fluid. They are there to suit you and your wants and needs, because you, above all else, matter.

You might also have different boundaries for different relationships and different people may set different boundaries for you. You'll hopefully start to get a feel for what's right for you the more you practice clearly stating your needs.

'Real' life vs online

These days, many of us have social and professional connections both in the 'real' world and online. Online relationships can be particularly tricky. People say and do things from behind the relative anonymity of a screen that they would never say or do in person. People have different communication styles which can lead to miscommunication, especially online where you don't have any clues from someone's body language, facial expressions or tone of voice.

As with all of your relationships, look for online connections that nurture and support you rather than those that weigh you down with negativity or unfair expectations. If you're not sure what someone means because of the missing nuances of online conversations, ask for clarification.

It might sound harsh but when was the last time you gave your social media accounts a good purge?

Are you spending time in Facebook groups that no longer serve you? Do you censor what you say because you're worried about certain people's opinions? Or does following someone, famous or not, make you feel bad about yourself or stress you out?

Again, it's OK to walk away if you've outgrown certain groups or relationships. I did exactly that over a couple of days during the 2020 Coronavirus lockdown. I unfollowed people online, unfriended them, unsubscribed and deleted emails, deleted photos and just had a whole online cleanse. It was so liberating! I really do suggest doing something along these lines if you feel there is too much noise out there every time you go online.

Are you a fixer?

I didn't want to end this chapter without talking about one issue that I think affects a lot of relationships and that's the need to play the role of 'fixer' or 'saviour'. Without wanting to make too many sweeping statements, I notice that a lot of women feel that it's their responsibility to 'fix' everything for the people they care about. As lovely as this seems, and although it comes from a kind place, if you actually move from top level thinking and delve a little deeper you will realise that this can have dire consequences on both sides of a relationship.

If you're a fixer, you'll probably recognise the scenario below.

When a friend/family member/colleague comes to you with a problem your natural instinct is to dive right in and come up with a solution for them. You want to give them advice, reassure them by telling them a story about when you were in a similar situation or take the problem off their hands.

If you don't have an immediate solution, you may feel so bad about it that the next thing to come out of your mouth is 'What can I do to help you?'

or 'How can I make you feel better?'

Sound familiar?

By doing this you believe you're being a good friend but think about it this way, by stepping in and taking control, by becoming the hero of the hour and not allowing the other person to be their own saviour, you're doing them an injustice and, in the long-run, setting them up for a fall.

By taking away the chance for them to take charge and come up with their own solution they become more and more dependent on you doing it for them. You're sending a deep, unconscious message to the other person – even though it's not your intention – that 'you're not capable of dealing with this' or 'I can do this quicker, easier, better than you can'. In turn, they increasingly rely on you to fix their problems, no matter how often it happens or however big or small that new problem may be.

This sets a pattern, disempowering the other person and leaving you feeling unfairly 'put upon'.

I found myself in this position from quite a young age. A natural problem solver, I was often the friend that people went to for advice and that followed me through to adult life. It was also one of the hardest things I found to work on, after all it is never going to be easy to change a behaviour of 30-plus years, especially when I believed it was one of my best qualities.

I am naturally a very empathetic person who can't bear to see someone struggling (I mean I cry at any charity advert no matter how many times I have seen it!) but it's even harder for me to see someone I care about struggle.

As I got older and more self-aware, I realised that fixing other people's problems was literally starting to take over my life. I would lose sleep worrying about them or cancel plans I had been looking forward to in order to fix them. At times, I couldn't focus on my own reality because I was so distracted by others and I often went without financially, energetically and emotionally to make their problems disappear.

It was somewhat manageable when I had a small group of friends but as my circles grew bigger, it got harder and harder to get through a day where I wasn't fixing a problem for someone else. There wasn't a day when I wouldn't get a call, a visit or a message that ultimately ended up in my giving some sort of advice or trying to solve some sort of problem.

Does any of this resonate with you? Have you been in this position too?

If so, here are some of the ways I managed to give the control back to the people I loved and allowed them to figure out how to help themselves.

I started by acknowledging that I had actually been taking the power away from the people I cared about. Next, I realised that I needed to change how we were communicating. I also needed to push back against people relying on me for instant advice.

I stopped jumping in with solutions or asking how I could fix the problem for them. Instead, I learned to make room for them to find their voice and tap into their instincts. I did this by asking questions like, 'What do you think would be the best solution?' and 'What could you do to fix this?'

In fact, questions are everything when you want to step out of the 'fixer' role. I learned to ask questions like:

* Have you had a similar problem in the past? If so, how did you solve it?

* What would happen if you did nothing?

* If you knew it would work out, what would you like to try?

* If I came to you with the same problem, what would you advise me to do? (This is my favourite one.)

* What have you already tried?

* What could you do differently?

* Could there be ways that you're contributing to this problem, perhaps unintentionally?

The secret here is to throw the questions back to the other person to encourage them to draw on their own instincts.

A harsh reality that I had to own as a long-time fixer is that solving problems for other people is actually more about our egos than the other person's needs. It can also feed into a sense of martyrdom – 'I always have to do everything for everyone' – which supports the belief that you have to sacrifice your needs for others.

Many people put themselves at the bottom of their list because they believe that their loved ones can't cope without them.

In my experience, it's better to give people opportunities to solve their own problems. This kind of empowerment and support is how personalities and relationships thrive and how we can truly make a positive difference to those we care about. At the same time we regain time and energy to put ourselves higher up on our priority list.

Some people aren't good at asking for help because they're so used to being 'the helper'.

Throughout their life, they've experienced an unbalanced give and take, so their instinct is usually 'I'll figure it out on my own'.

Check in on the 'helpers' in your life.

- Unknown

REFLECTION TIME

How do you feel?

_____

_____

_____

What have you learnt?

_____

_____

_____

What will you change?

_____

_____

_____

What will you do more of?

_____

_____

_____

What will you do less of?

_____

_____

_____

Does this raise any strong feelings for you?
(This is your gut telling you that there's a potential issue you need to address)

_____

_____

_____

Do you have any questions?

_____

_____

_____

Chapter 11:

Control the controllables

(Control the things you can control & learn
how to cope with the things you can't)

In my opinion, there are three very important words that hold the secret to a much less stressful and more fulfilling life. Want to know what they are?

Control the controllables.

By focusing on that approach to life you'll instantly feel like a ten-tonne weight has lifted from your shoulders. Believe me, I have lived it.

The thing about controlling the controllables is that it takes you from a victim mindset – everything happens to me and I don't get a say – to an empowered mindset – I can't influence what other people do but I can control how I behave and how I respond.

Let's imagine a situation where you believe someone has been gossiping about you at work, suggesting to your new manager that your mind isn't always on the job because you have young children in nursery. Naturally, it feels unfair. You want the person to stop and for her and your manager to see how hard you work, as well as the quality of what you do. You want to feel respected and valued and for people to say good things about you.

While it's completely understandable that you want all of these things to happen, none of them are in your control. You can't stop people gossiping, you can't guarantee that people will say good things, you can't even control whether or not your new manager values you.

Constantly wanting others to change is a dangerous and stressful way to live. If your happiness depends entirely on things you can't control, then you will always be at the mercy of other people's reactions or decisions.

You deserve so much more than this!

So, in this scenario, what can you control?

Well, you can ensure that you go into meetings well-prepared. You can deliver high quality work. You can request a meeting with your new manager and explain that your nursery has a policy of issuing fines to parents who are late for pick up, which is why you need to leave on time, but also talk about all the ways in which you're committed to your job and present throughout the day.

The key here is to switch from focusing on how you want another person to think/feel/speak/behave to concentrating on how you think/feel/speak/behave.

The only things that you can control are what you think, feel, say or do.

Other examples spring to mind too.

For example, you can't control what other people think when your toddler is throwing a massive tantrum in the supermarket or when your dog is barking at another dog on the other side of the road. You can only control how you respond to and cope with those situations.

You can't control being stuck in traffic, but you can control making sure the car is full of petrol, leaving with time to spare or packing snacks for a protracted journey.

You can't control the friendships your children make at school, but you can be there to provide a listening ear in the event of a falling out.

Stop worrying about what you can't control

Worrying about what you can't control is distracting. It holds you back and slows you down. It's like walking around with an umbrella constantly held above your head, just in case it rains.

There are so many things that can take up our headspace and so many things on a day-to-day basis that we need to turn our attention and thoughts to without using it all up to think about the things that 'could happen'.

I'm writing this book in the middle of the coronavirus pandemic.

There's so much HUGE stuff happening in the world right now and I could let it consume my thoughts and feelings. After all, I have three businesses that employ over 20 staff and bills that still need paying, regardless of whether there is money coming in or not (which there wasn't for two of the businesses for a while, by the way). We had to temporarily close the doors to the salon for four months and the flooring business for over a month when lockdown hit. At the same time, I was trying to keep two kids safe and sane as well as attempting to home-school them, not something I enjoyed at all, even if I do hold a degree in Childhood Studies!

But, honestly, how much of it is under my control? Very little! All I can do is control how I behave and respond and how I use my time. And writing this book feels like a good, proactive use of my energy.

The truth is that sometimes we just have to tap into our inner Queen Elsa and let it go. We have to recognise when things are beyond our influence and focus back on what we do have power over.

Activity Twelve: Find your controllables

In this activity, I want you to write down anything you're worrying about at the moment. Think about the things that are keeping you awake at night – anything counts, no matter how big or how small.

Leave a line in between each one.

Give yourself ten minutes. Go!

You can use the space over the page or print out a worksheet at:

https://www.jobevilacqua.com/resources/

FIND YOUR CONTROLLABLES

Write down anything you're worrying about at the moment.
Think about the things that are keeping you awake at night – anything counts, no
matter how big or how small.

_____

_____

_____

_____

_____

_____

_____

_____

_____

_____

_____

_____

_____

_____

Identify what you can control

Looking at your list, I want you to put a mark of some kind (a tick, star or green dot would work well) against all the things on your list that you could potentially control by changing what you think, feel, say or do.

Be as honest as you can. Fear or lack of confidence may be holding you back. You may feel like you can't control something when actually you can. Jot down some action points underneath each worry (that's why I asked you to leave a line) with some ideas of what you could do.

Coping with what you can't control

What worries are left on your list? These are probably the things over which you feel you have no control. How can you deal with them?

There are so many things in life we can't control, from tiny inconveniences to massive life-changing tragedies. We can't control what people think or how they feel. We can't always control who we work with or who our boss is, or who our children hang out with or how they want to spend their time.

You can waste months or even years of your life wishing things were different and that you could control all of these things but, truth bomb, you can't. Honestly, your energy could be so much better spent elsewhere.

If you're one of the many struggling with things beyond your control right now, why not try these tips:

• Feel your feelings

Just because something is beyond your control doesn't mean you don't feel it. One of the most powerful things you can do is sit with your feelings when they happen rather than trying to bury them.

Tell yourself the truth. Out loud or in a journal.

It's OK to say, 'I'm just really hurt that he/she laughed at me. I feel sad and embarrassed'.

- Take deep breaths

Feeling overwhelmed or out of control can literally knock the breath out of us. Deep, calming breaths can help you to relax. They're also a reminder that your breathing is something you can control.

Try this: place one hand on your belly button. Inhale through your nose, so your belly expands out and fills with air, like a balloon. Exhale, so your belly moves inward. As you inhale, tell yourself that you're breathing in health and healing and on the exhale that you're breathing out any worries and concerns.

- Don't fixate on the reasons

Sometimes, things happen in life that feel very unfair, don't they? It's even worse when it's something you can't control. It's easy to get caught up in a cycle of blame and looking for reasons, 'Maybe the relationship wouldn't have ended if I wanted to go out more', or 'He might not have sprained his ankle if I'd have stopped him playing on the trampoline'. All this thinking does is trap you and make you feel bad. The reality is that uncontrollable things happen.

The only way to move forward is to either let them go or decide what you can do that's within your sphere of control.

- Turn to someone you trust

When you feel out of control, it's tempting to withdraw. However, this may be precisely the time that you need someone stable and trustworthy in your corner to help you pinpoint the things you do have control over.

I feel blessed that there are a few people I know I can call on for help and advice. However, there is one person in particular who I can ring and who will listen to me for five minutes or five hours, no matter what I'm thinking or feeling. She will help me process my thoughts and ground me so that I can see clearly and lead with logic, not just emotion.

She is my anchor and I hope that you have at least one person like her that you can call in times of need and who can remind you of what you can and can't control.

• Remind yourself that nothing lasts forever

No matter how horrible it feels to have things in your life that you can't control, take a moment to remind yourself that nothing is permanent. Tough situations won't last forever, no matter how much they may feel like they will at the time you're going through it.

If there is something you can positively influence, it's OK to take small steps. Be gentle and kind to yourself. Think about what you can realistically do in the moment.

As for the rest? This too will pass.

And remember, you have survived all the other bad stuff that has happened to you before. You will get over anything else coming your way because you are way stronger than you think, I know you are.

What other people think of you is none of your business

Something else I really want to impress upon you is that it isn't your responsibility to control other people's reactions to your choices.

It's so tempting to believe that, if people are unhappy with something we've said or done, then we must be in the wrong. This usually isn't the case.

As we talked about in Chapter 8, other people's expectations mean they see us in a certain way but it's more about what they want or feel themselves than what we're about. Other people's reactions to your decisions are about their expectations, self-esteem and insecurities, and honestly, that's none of your business. You've got enough of your own stuff to worry about right now, like getting yourself at the top of your own priority list!

It's up to the other person to manage their own feelings about your choices. It isn't your job to make yourself smaller, hold yourself back or make yourself unhappy to make other people feel better. Nope, not on my watch, lady!

Remember, the only things that you can control are what you think, feel, say or do. Everything else is irrelevant.

REFLECTION TIME

How do you feel?

_____

_____

_____

What have you learnt?

_____

_____

_____

What will you change?

_____

_____

_____

What will you do more of?

_____

_____

_____

What will you do less of?

_____

_____

_____

Does this raise any strong feelings for you?
(This is your gut telling you that there's a potential issue you need to address)

_____

_____

_____

Do you have any questions?

_____

_____

_____

There are hundreds of thousands of versions of you that exist in the minds of others. There are going to be versions of us that exist that people don't like no matter what we do.

When we understand this, and I mean truly understand it, the true, raw, authentic and not-giving-a-shit-what-people-think version of you comes out to play.

- @matt_cama

Chapter 12:

Finding your voice

(How to feel confident about communicating your wants and needs)

As you've been working through this book, I hope you've been starting to build a clearer sense of who you are and what you want in life, as well as what you don't want.

The next stage is to make the leap from thinking about what you want to actually making it happen. One of the biggest barriers to this is a lack of self-confidence and/or self-esteem.

It can be even harder if you're worried that certain people in your life might not support you in stating and pursuing your needs.

How do you find your voice when you're not sure what you want to say yet? Or when you know that what you have to say won't please everyone?

Surround yourself with the right people

There's a quote from world-famous motivational speaker Jim Rohn that says, 'You are the average of the five people you spend the most time with'.

The people we spend time with determine which conversations dominate our attention. They affect the behaviours and attitudes to which we're regularly exposed. With time, most of us start to reflect our closest relationships in the way we think and behave.

This can, of course, be incredibly empowering if you are surrounded by positive and uplifting people but if you're always around negative people who bring you and your mood down, then that can be incredibly debilitating.

Don't think the people you hang around with have much influence? According to research by social psychologist, Dr David McClelland of Harvard, the people you habitually associate with 'determine as much as 95 per cent of your success or failure in life'[9].

That's a HUGE figure, don't you think?

Let's take a minute to think about the people around you, in your life right now. Do they lift you up? Are they your biggest cheerleaders? Do they believe you can do anything you set your mind to?

Or are they holding you back? Do they weigh you down with negativity? Are they always creating roadblocks in your life or shouting down your dreams?

Before you can truly find your voice and have the confidence to use it, you may need to make some difficult decisions about certain relationships, even if it's just to have a hard conversation where you reset the boundaries, the boundaries that are going to make you happier and ride up that priority list of yours.

It might sound brutal but I believe that sometimes we outgrow certain relationships in our lives, and that when we do, it's acceptable to walk away or, at the very least, minimise the amount of contact you have with those people.

What I've learned from my own experiences is that the right people in your life will support your choices and adapt to accommodate them. It isn't always an overnight thing but, most importantly, there's a willingness to move in the right direction. There's also a belief that both parties in the relationship deserve to live the best versions of their lives.

If you're really struggling with relationships that are turning the volume down on your voice or distorting what you say, then I'd urge you to go back and give Chapter 10: Relationships a re-read.

You've got this!

Own your choices

Remember how in Chapter 11 we were talking about controlling the controllables? Well, that is very relevant when it comes to finding your own voice.

Sometimes, people will disagree with what you have to say or the choices you make. That doesn't mean you're in the wrong. As scary as it is, it's crucial to own your decisions and to accept that you can't control other people's reactions or opinions.

Use your voice regardless of their opinions of your own choices.

Building confidence

One of the biggest reasons it can be hard to speak up for what you want and own your choices is a lack of confidence. I want to spend the rest of this chapter looking at some great confidence-building strategies as we have touched on it a lot in this book.

The first thing to recognise is that building self-confidence takes effort. Sometimes A LOT of effort.

It's easy to assume that some people are born with confidence and that you just missed the boat, genetically-speaking. In reality, confident people with good self-esteem weren't born that way. They may, however, have had confident role models in their early lives, such as parents who taught them confidence-building behaviours in childhood.

If that wasn't your experience, it doesn't mean there's no hope.

You can create confidence. It just takes practice.

This is possible for you too.

What I've found is that confidence comes from repeating small successes over and over again and then building them into larger successes. This is because every time we do something well or we experience a good outcome, it gives our brain positive messages about our capabilities.

When we start to see ourselves as capable, we begin to feel more confident.

Confidence-building strategies

Below, you'll find some of my favourite confidence-building strategies and exercises. My advice is to keep experimenting with different approaches until you find the strategies that begin to feel more natural to you.

1.   Smile and look people in the eye

People who make frequent, gentle eye contact (not intense, threatening stares!) are perceived by others as being more warm, personable, attractive, likeable, qualified, skilled, competent and valuable, more trustworthy, honest, sincere, more confident and emotionally stable than people who struggle to look others in the eye.

Smiles are equally as powerful. Other people view those who smile easily as more confident and attractive[10]. Looking at a smiling face releases endorphins making the person being smiled at feel happier and more relaxed.

Smiling is great for you too. When we smile, it triggers a loop where we feedback joy, and endorphins, to the brain, which then prompts more smiling and so on. In fact, one study found that smiling can be as stimulating to our brains as receiving £16,000 in cash or 2,000 chocolate bars[11]. How AMAZING is that?!

So, from today, I'd love you to greet the world with a smile and some gentle eye contact. Say 'Good morning' and smile as you walk past people on the pavement. Smile at shop assistants, bus drivers, receptionists or the person in the park walking their dog. Give your kids some extra big smiles throughout the day.

The more smiles you receive back, the happier you'll feel, thanks to all the bliss-inducing endorphins.

2. Give genuine compliments

Life can be tough. Sometimes it gets so tough that we stop seeing the good in the people and circumstances around us.

One way to feel more positive, optimistic and – you guessed it – confident is to give genuine compliments to other people. Giving positive feedback will shift your mindset to focus on good things and, through little acts of love and kindness, change how you feel about yourself.

The key is to ensure your compliments come from the heart. Tell someone that their smile lights up the room or that the colour they're wearing suits them. Tell them that you value their perspective or that the world is a better place because they're in it.

Amazingly, the more you give out confidence to others, the more it will grow inside of you.

And if someone compliments you? Please, please, PLEASE don't brush it off! Instead, I want you to practice saying, 'Thank you' and letting the compliment settle inside of you.

3. Practice appreciation/gratitude

Has anyone ever suggested that you keep a gratitude diary/journal? This can actually be a really powerful practice.

These days, many cognitive behaviour therapists, for example, will encourage people facing mental health challenges or low self-esteem to write a daily gratitude journal. Research shows benefits such as better sleep, fewer symptoms of illness and higher levels of happiness[12].

The idea is that you write a list of five things in your journal for which you're grateful. This should be done at least once a week but could be something you practice every day. You don't need to write much, just five short sentences that reflect the things you appreciate in your current life.

Entries could include anything from 'waking up this morning' or 'having the strength in my legs to go for a walk' to 'the kindness of my friends', 'the sun shining' or 'listening to my favourite album'. Write down whatever those five things are for you that day.

The act of writing down the things you appreciate is proven to deepen their emotional impact and to change the wiring of your brain to focus more on what you have rather than what you lack.

4.   *Play to your strengths*

As I've mentioned above, confidence comes from banking as many successes as possible. One of the most effective ways to do this is to play to your strengths.

We all have things we're good at in life, as well as things that don't come easily. More importantly, there are some things that make time fly (a valuable clue that something lights you up inside) and some things that feel like an eternity in hell!

I want you to give yourself permission to do more of the things that play to your strengths. Seek out activities that suit your knowledge, talents and skill set. Also do the things you love, even if you suck at them at the moment. You can always get better!

Again, the purpose here is to keep giving your brain positive messages about what you can do rather than what you can't. I want you to feel good about how you spend your time.

You can always outsource or delegate tasks that don't suit you. Those tasks might be a nightmare for you, but they could be a perfect fit for someone else.

This is a lesson I've had to learn while running three businesses. The truth is that no-one can be amazing at everything. If I focus on doing the stuff that I'm good at, I can get so much more done than I would by struggling through things that aren't my forte or I just don't enjoy. And I can feel happy and confident about my choices.

5. Get things done

As we looked at earlier in this chapter, confidence is built on small successes that turn into bigger successes. In other words, it's built on accomplishment. This is why I'm such a fan of goal setting (see Chapter 17).

It's time to show yourself that you are someone capable of getting things done.

Try this:

* Every morning, set yourself one big goal for the day – the non-negotiable thing you must get done.

* Below it, write down three smaller but achievable goals for the same day.

* At the beginning of the month, write down three slighter bigger goals for the month ahead.

Your small daily goals could be things that work towards achieving one of your bigger monthly goals.

Track what you do. Write down your goals and take great pleasure from crossing them out when you achieve them. You could even list your achievements and pin them up somewhere.

The aim here is to begin reframing yourself as someone who knows what they want to achieve and takes action to get things done.

6.   *Ignore the naysayers!*

There will always be people who tell you that you can't accomplish your goals or who will try to drown out your voice.

You absolutely CANNOT and MUST NOT listen to them!

Even when people tell you the odds are against you, remember that there are people in the world who achieve extraordinary things every day, despite everyone telling them it couldn't be done.

If I had listened to other people, I would never have opened Serenity Loves, I would never have created my amazing woman's community She Leads and I certainly wouldn't be writing this book right now. People succeed all the time. Why shouldn't/couldn't/wouldn't you be one of those people?

Just because your choices aren't right for someone else, doesn't mean they aren't right for you. And that's all that matters.

Activity Thirteen: Find your voice

This exercise is all about finding out more about who you are and what truly matters to you.

Try not to overthink your answers too much. The longer you spend on it, the greater the chances are that you'll censor what you really think in favour of other people's opinions.

So, find a quiet place again and grab a pen. I want you to answer these ten questions, writing down as much as you can. Try to spend at least 30 minutes on this (an hour would be even better but I know quiet hours may sound as fictitious as a sparkly unicorn delivering that chocolate ice cream that helps you lose weight.)

FIND YOUR VOICE

What angers you? (Think about the big picture stuff in society.)

What makes you cry?

What have you mastered? (i.e. what can you do well without having to think about it?)

What gives you hope?

As a child, what did you want to be when you grew up? (This is often where the clues to our true voice sit – who were you before you became burdened with the expectations of others?)

If you had all the time and money in the world, what would you do?

What would blow your mind with joy/excitement if it happened? (List as many things as you can.)

If you were going to express yourself creatively, what would you prefer to do? (e.g. write a poem or novel, paint, sculpt, play music, etc.)

What change would you like to see in the world?

If you had one day left to live, how would you spend it?

The answers to the questions above will hopefully give you better insights into what makes you tick, what motivates you, what puts a fire in your belly and what you want to use your voice to say.

The more you love your decisions, the less you need others to love them.

- Unknown

REFLECTION TIME

How do you feel?

_____

_____

_____

What have you learnt?

_____

_____

_____

What will you change?

_____

_____

_____

What will you do more of?

_____

_____

_____

What will you do less of?

_____

_____

_____

Does this raise any strong feelings for you?
(This is your gut telling you that there's a potential issue you need to address)

_____

_____

_____

Do you have any questions?

_____

_____

_____

Chapter 13:

Knowing your worth

(It's time to be unapologetically you)

I want you to take a deep breath and ask yourself …

Am I worthy?

If your answer was anything but a resounding 'YES!' then this chapter is for you.

Many people hear this question and try to rationalise it by saying, 'What do you mean by worthy? What's the context? Am I worthy of what?'

Or you might be one of the people that says, 'Well, I might be worthy some of the time … perhaps I'm worthy of some of the good things in my life.'

And I bet a lot of you reading this say, 'Hmmm, dunno.'

But it's time to flip your thinking. It's time for you to start seeing yourself as worthy. If you can do that, you will stop undervaluing yourself and start prioritising your needs more.

I believe that we are all innately worthy. If I asked everyone reading this book whether babies come into this world worthy, I bet 99.9% of you would agree that they do. Therefore, I know that you came into this world worthy of all the good things that life has to offer. So, when did that change? When did you stop being worthy? Was it at five years old? 10? 20? 30?

The truth is you never stopped being worthy! You always have been and always will be worthy. And I'm truly sorry if you have ever believed or felt otherwise.

Our fast-paced life doesn't always lend us the time to think about who we are and what we bring to this world. As we've seen so far in this book, lots of different factors can come together to chip away at your sense of self-worth and confidence.

Relationships, expectations, pressure, circumstances. Throw them all into the mix and I'm not surprised that so many of us end up losing ourselves and believing that we're not worthy of good things, or that other people's needs are more important than our own.

I bet you find it far, far easier to think about all the ways in which you 'lack' rather than your many wonderful strengths, qualities and talents you hold.

Enough!

It's time to start celebrating and being unapologetically, marvellously YOU!

This chapter is all about how you can go from lost to found. How you can become more self-aware and truly start to celebrate what makes you a special, one-of-a-kind, in this world of 7.8 billion people.

The relationship you have with yourself is the most complicated one because you can't walk away from YOU.

You have to forgive every mistake and deal with every flaw. You have to find a way to love you even when you are disgusted with you.

- Unknown

Looking back over your journey

First of all, I want you to think about the journey that has brought you to where you are today. If you had to present the key highlights and milestones – the CliffsNotes of your life – what would they be? Think about your personal and professional experiences.

For example, my potted history might be:

* Self-confessed party girl in my early 20s

* Met and married my husband

* Founded Hallmark Carpets and Flooring in 2009 with my husband while on maternity leave – learned a lot about running a successful business (and made plenty of mistakes!)

* Founded Serenity Loves – a beauty salon with supervised crèche – when pregnant with my second daughter in 2011

* Mum to two beautiful girls

* Grew two successful businesses and expanded team, doubling the workforce

* Founded Jo Bevilacqua (formerly The Unique Mumpreneur) in 2017 to support other entrepreneurs to build their businesses

This pretty much only covers my professional journey. I could have thrown plenty more personal milestones in there too but, to be honest, that probably would have taken up the book in itself and definitely wouldn't have been so positive either. The milestones would have been filled with failed relationships (both platonic and romantic), financial hardships and a host of other crazy episodes that are best left where they are, not in the public arena.

Your milestones might be completely different or similar, full of happy and not so happy moments. They might include challenges like postnatal depression, injury or illness, redundancy, relationships ending, caring for others, bereavement, etc. as well as achievements such as qualifications, promotions, career changes, artistic endeavours, successful relationships or having a child.

No two journeys will ever be the same.

But what I know is that whatever brought you to this point, your journey has helped to shape the unique, amazing person you are today. I want you to look at your journey and see how even the toughest points tell you something good about yourself.

Scan back over all of the activities you've done in this book so far. They will tell you a lot about your journey too.

Recognise your skills

As you look over the key stages in your life, I want you to start thinking about what skills and knowledge these events and experiences have given you.

The skills might not be immediately obvious so you may need to think outside of the box.

Don't put yourself down.

It's so easy to think about things like organising family life, helping your kids with their homework, running a house on one wage and starting a business in blind faith, and believe that these are skills everyone has.

Give yourself some credit! Your ability to do these things really matters. Recognise just how capable you are and what those skills could mean for you.

Do you remember those British Army Reserves adverts that were about taking your skills from civilian life and using them in the Reserves at the weekends? They were all about recognising transferable skills.

For example, if you're really good at budgeting at home for your family, you could have exactly the right skills to be an accountant or manage a budget in some capacity at work. If you organise incredible birthday parties for your kids, you could have what it takes to be a party planner or event organiser. If you find yourself learning about dog behaviour after bringing a rescue dog home, perhaps you have it in you to qualify as a force-free dog behaviourist.

It's amazing where different skills, interests and experiences can take you. You just have to give yourself permission to be open to it.

Activity Fourteen: SWOT analysis

Grab a pen. For our next activity, I want you to do a SWOT analysis. If you've ever worked in the corporate world or you already run your own business, you might be an old hand at these. If you're not, don't worry! I've got you covered.

What is a SWOT analysis?

Well, SWOT stands for Strengths, Weakness, Opportunities and Threats. It's a great exercise for identifying what you're great at, how you can move towards your goals, gaps in your skills and potential derailers.

Using the table over the page as a prompt, I want you to jot down as many points as you can answering the questions in each box.

I would encourage you to dig deep and complete it yourself, although if you do struggle you might need to ask your friends and family what they think you're good at. Sometimes it takes other people to see your talents before you can notice them but, by now, I would hope that you believe in yourself enough to be able to fill it out with little difficulty.

As you're filling out the SWOT analysis, go back to your journey and think about those all-important transferable skills you have accumulated over the years, there will be LOADS.

Strengths

What advantages do you have that others don't have (e.g. skills, certifications, education, or connections)?

What do you do better than anyone else?

What personal resources can you access?

What do other people see as your strengths?

Which of your achievements are you most proud of?

Are you part of a network? If so, what connections do you have that could help and support you?

Weaknesses

What tasks do you usually avoid because you don't feel confident doing them?

What do other people see as your weaknesses?

Are you completely confident in your education and skills training? If not, where are you weakest?

What are your negative habits (e.g. are you often late, are you disorganised, do you have a short temper, or are you poor at handling stress)?

Do you have personality traits that hold you back in your field? For instance, if you have to conduct meetings on a regular basis, a fear of public speaking would be a major weakness.

Opportunities

What new technology can help you? Or can you get help from others or from people via the internet?

Do you have a network of strategic contacts to help you, or offer good advice?

What trends do you see around you, and how can you take advantage of them?

If you want to run your own business, for example, can you see a gap that no-one else is filling?

Threats

What external factors could derail your plans/dreams because you have no control over them?

What obstacles do you face?

Could any of your weaknesses stop you from achieving your goals?

If we KNOW who we are, we can GROW who we are

I read once that humans fight an ongoing battle between being the person we wish to be and the person we really are. If we can become more self-aware, perhaps we can begin to close the gap between the two.

Greater self-awareness will help you develop a greater sense of self-worth. You have as much right to good things in life as anyone else in the world. Once you believe this, you will stop putting yourself last on the list.

So, how can you grow your self-awareness?

1.   Be honest about your strengths and weaknesses

This was what the SWOT analysis was about. Knowing your strengths can help you spot opportunities and knowing your weaknesses can help you fill the gaps that have been holding you back.

2.   Ask yourself the difficult questions

This book so far has been about getting you to consider the difficult questions in life like, What would you do if you knew you couldn't fail? What are your values, beliefs and goals?

3.   Learn from your mistakes

Self-awareness is a matter of life-long learning. As we've explored in earlier chapters, you will make mistakes in life, we all do, it's part and parcel of growing up. It's what you take away from those mistakes that matters. Reflect on what happened, what you could do differently next time, and don't forget to acknowledge what you did well.

4.   Try new things

You will learn more about your capabilities each time you try something new and step outside of your comfort zone. You don't have to try huge, life-changing new things like leaping out of a plane or ditching your job to travel the world. Small things can make a big difference.

5.   Recall your natural strengths and interests

What did you love when you were a child? What did you do well? What did you want to be? What did you role play? How did you most enjoy spending your time?

Often, the things we are naturally drawn to, especially before other people's expectations weigh down on us, are the things that light us up inside.

6.   Learn from your past

Most of us have a blueprint for life. We gravitate towards certain people and repeat certain patterns of behaviour. Not all of them are healthy. If you keep finding yourself in the same situation time and again, it might be time to break the cycle once and for all.

7.   Gather resources

Again, we've already talked about collecting quotes, pictures, evidence, etc. that support the positive changes you want to make in your life. If, for example, there's a person who seems to embody a trait you would like to have, find out as much as you can about them and learn from them.

8.   Claim time for yourself

I know you're busy. I know you barely have a moment to think some days. But, if you're going to stop putting yourself last on the list, it's time to carve out a bit of time for yourself every day. Just 15 minutes a day working towards a goal will add up to an hour and three quarters a week, seven hours a month and nearly four whole days and nights a year dedicated entirely to bettering your life.

Are you being appreciated?

Looking at your strengths and all the things you have achieved in your life so far, I think you'll see a person who is worthy of good things.

I want you to remind yourself of those strengths every day. Write them down. Pin them next to your mirror or on your kitchen noticeboard. Read them often. Better yet, say them out loud!

If you don't feel like your loved ones appreciate you, the chances are that they're following your example and that you don't appreciate yourself enough. It's time to start demanding more of yourself and for yourself.

To coin the legendary phrase from L'Oreal …

Because you're worth it.

There will always be someone who can't see your worth.

Don't let it be you.

- *Unknown*

REFLECTION TIME

How do you feel?

_____

_____

_____

What have you learnt?

_____

_____

_____

What will you change?

_____

_____

_____

What will you do more of?

_____

_____

_____

What will you do less of?

_____

_____

_____

Does this raise any strong feelings for you?
(This is your gut telling you that there's a potential issue you need to address)

_____

_____

_____

Do you have any questions?

_____

_____

_____

Chapter 14:

Building a business or getting that promotion

(How to get what you want from your career)

Writer Annie Dillard famously said, 'How we spend our days is, of course, how we spend our lives.'

For many of us, a large portion of our days is spent at work. In fact, the average person will spend 90,000 hours at work over a lifetime[13]. That equates to about a third of our lives! That's a lot of time to spend on something that doesn't light you up inside.

So, be honest with me, how do you feel about work right now?

Do you leap out of bed in the mornings excited about the day ahead, or are you wishing your days away, living for the weekend and getting that horrible 'back-to-school' feeling on Sunday evenings?

Life's too short to wish it away.

In this chapter, we're going to start thinking about how you can shape your career in a way that makes you feel fulfilled and happy to get out of bed in the mornings.

This will look different for everyone. It might mean creating a business, getting that promotion you've always wanted or changing careers altogether. It might even mean scaling back your work to spend more time on other pursuits.

You're in the driving seat.

What do you want from your career?

Do you love what you do and want to do more of it? Are you yearning to secure a big promotion? Or are you sick of working for someone else and want to go it alone by setting up your own business?

The first step is to get crystal clear on what you would want to achieve if nothing was holding you back. If you think about your ideal future career, where do you see yourself?

Step two is to map out a plan to make it happen.

Activity Fifteen: Your dream career

Grab a pen! For the next ten minutes, I want you to write down absolutely everything that you could gain from pursuing a new job or business if you could punch your way through your fear.

I KNOW you're probably thinking about all the things that could go wrong but trust me, there is so much that could go right. Take it from someone who has created three successful businesses. You wouldn't believe how much fear I've felt each time, but I truly believe that the benefits outweigh the fear.

So, go on, write down all the ways your life could change for the better if you felt more fulfilled in your career. These could be emotional benefits, financial benefits, a better lifestyle – whatever motivates you. Let yourself dream big.

Go!

YOUR DREAM CAREER

Write down absolutely everything that you could gain from pursuing a new job or
business if you could punch your way through your fear.

_____

_____

_____

_____

_____

_____

_____

_____

_____

_____

_____

_____

_____

_____

_____

_____

_____

Women need a seat at the table. They need an invitation to be seated there and, in some cases, where this is not available, they need to create their own table.

- Meghan Markle

Shifting your mindset

How did it feel to think about all the things that could go right if you start pursuing a career or business that you love?

We talked about creating a vision board earlier in the book, didn't we? So, you might have a board that's entirely focused on the outcomes you want for your working life or you might just have reserved part of your vision board for your career. Either way, that's ok.

Remember, it's about what a happy, fulfilling job/career/business looks like to you. It could be that you want to work just 10 hours a week, you want to retrain, get promoted, take a step back or launch a new product.

There's no right or wrong here – only what's right for you.

Do we demand too much of ourselves?

You may still feel like something is holding you back.

As I expect that it will be mostly women reading this book (but hello to any guys who are on this journey too!), I thought it would be a good idea to look at how gender can influence our mindset about stepping up the work ladder.

It would appear that women set themselves very high standards for taking the next step in their careers.

In 2019, LinkedIn's Gender Insights Report[14] highlighted the glaring differences between how men and women approach finding a new job. I wish I could say that I was shocked by the report but, really, all it did was confirm my own observations.

Here are the big takeaway stats:

* 90% of men and women are open to hearing about new job opportunities

from recruiters and their networks

* Both genders view an average of 45 jobs per candidate and both do a similar amount of research into each job

But this is where the similarities end!

* Women are 16% less likely than men to apply for a job after viewing it

* Women apply for 20% fewer jobs than men

And here's the big difference in mindset:

* Men tend to apply for a job if they feel they fulfil 60% of the criteria whereas **women only apply if they feel they meet 100%!**

* Women are also 26% less likely to ask for a referral than men

That's some pretty high standards we women set for ourselves.

This means we're proactively adding to the gender bias within the jobs market, or maybe we expect so much of ourselves because we've experienced gender bias first-hand. We want to give employers as little chance to say no as possible.

The report found that recruiters are 13% less likely to look at a woman's profile on LinkedIn if she comes up in a candidate search, which is maybe one of the reasons that women feel they have to be able to nail a role before they can apply for it.

The good news is that when women do apply for a job, they're 16% more likely to get hired than men. As we've seen though, this is probably because the women applying are highly qualified for their chosen role.

Interestingly, 68% of women want to know the salary range of a job before they will consider applying. There may be two significant reasons behind this:

1) Women tend to see organisations that are transparent about salaries as committed to fair pay.

2) Women often have to factor how their salary and work benefits will impact their wider family circumstances. For example, will they be able to afford childcare?

This report certainly gives us some food for thought.

Could you be holding back from applying for your dream job because you don't fit 100% of the job requirements?

If so, it's time to stop expecting perfection! Give yourself permission to step up your career!

How to land an interview when you don't meet 100% of the requirements

As we've seen, men are more likely to go for a job even if they don't meet all of the requirements. Being an employer myself, I strongly believe that you should always go for a job for which you know you'll be a great match, even if you can't tick every requirement box.

Personally, I think if you can already do everything that a job entails then it won't keep your interest for long. It's far better to stretch yourself and grow into a role – that's what keeps people motivated, not being able to do something with their eyes closed.

So, how can you land an interview for your dream job, even if you don't meet all of the requirements?

Try these tips:

1.   *Focus on your transferable skills*

You may need to look at the criteria for a job and think outside the box a bit. What skills are needed in order to fulfil the requirement?

For example, a job might ask for event planning experience. Even though you might not have that from work, what about the parties you've organised or all the planning that went into your wedding? Many of the same skills apply.

2.   Do a pre-interview project to showcase your skills

I recently read an interview with the CEO of a business who said he'd hired several people who didn't have the required expertise for a job because they were able to show they were a good fit. In his example, this guy said that he'd employed someone to be a product manager who'd never worked in product development. The interviewee had realised that the business wanted a great looking, functional and addictive digital product. The technical skills to create this (for example, HTML, CSS and Photoshop) could all be learned or outsourced at a later date.

What the interviewee did was take an existing product and put together a presentation covering 20 things they would change and why. They asked their friends for feedback and hired someone on Fiverr to mock-up new, improved product screens.

The interviewee stood out for their insights, creative vision and their passion, which spurred them to go the extra mile to secure the job.

3.   Find a direct connection

A lot of companies use software systems to filter job applications. If you're worried you don't tick enough boxes, another option is to ask for a referral or secure an interview through a direct contact at the company.

This is where your online and in-person networks can come into their own. Who do you know? And beyond that, who do they know? If you can find someone to make the introductions, you may be able to make your case for why you deserve an interview, even if you don't meet 100% of the criteria.

4.   Find out the job's non-negotiables

One article I read said that job descriptions are often a wish list of skills and knowledge rather than being set in stone. At the same time, every job probably has some non-negotiables, skills that are absolutely essential to being able to fulfil the role.

A great tip I came across a while back is to paste a job description into a word cloud app to see which words appear most prominently in the word cloud. These are probably the keywords that the applicant tracking system (ATS) has been told to use to flag up the best applications. You can then make sure that your application includes these non-negotiables.

5.   Pay attention to the language used

It's worth reading between the lines of a job description. It might say 'Social media marketing experience is desirable' but that doesn't mean it's essential. My guess is that this is a 'nice to have' rather than a deal breaker.

Look for these little variations in language or contradictions about the job requirements. The latter, for example, can be a sign that the job description has been copied and pasted from other roles and that the contradictory elements aren't essential.

How to ask for what you want at work – and actually get it!

Getting the career you want might just be about making more of the role you're in now or asking for more responsibility, recognition or opportunities in your current workplace.

I think many of us believe that if we work hard, our efforts will be recognised and rewarded. A tough lesson I've learned in life is that people are often so busy worrying about their own wants, needs or responsibilities that they may not give you what you want at work unless you actually ask for it.

As my kids recite back to me, often, 'If you don't ask, you don't get'.

Here are my top tips for making sure you have the confidence to ask and hopefully get the results you want:

1. Know why it matters

Whether you want a promotion, a pay rise, more holidays or more responsibility, you need to let your employer know what it's worth to you, why you're willing to stand up for it and why it should be yours.

Try to come up with three reasons to which it would be all but impossible to say no.

2. Be clear

Practice writing down what you want. Aim for just one or two clear and concise sentences that explain exactly what you're asking for. When you talk to your boss, you don't want there to be any ambiguity about what you want.

3. Ask the right person

Make sure you speak to the person within your organisation who has the power to give you what you want. Not your peers, not your colleagues, but the actual person who is going to make the decision.

4. Pick your time

Try to find a time when you can speak to the person you need to speak to without interruption. It's important to know that they're really listening and they don't feel distracted, hassled or cornered into making a decision.

5. Prepare for objections

Rather than an outright refusal, your request may be met with objections. Things like budget, time, the wider team, training, etc. are all common issues. Don't let this put you off! Objections are almost inevitable – your boss is doing their due diligence – and all the time they're raising objections, they're not saying, 'No'.

My advice is to think about what the objections could be in advance and go into your conversation with some planned counter-arguments.

6. Practice

Before you have a big conversation about what you want at work, it helps to practice. Write down what you want to say, why and any counter-arguments. Practice in front of the mirror. Run your request past your friends or even a trusted colleague.

Saying things out loud is completely different to having it written down. I would highly recommend the first time you say it out loud NOT be in front of the decision maker.

It can be a great confidence booster to know what you want to say and why fluently.

7. Don't be discouraged

Inevitably, there will be times when a work request is turned down. Try not to let this knock your confidence.

Instead, ask your boss if they could explain their reasoning or give you some pointers about what you would need to do to get a 'Yes' from them. Try to arrange a time for a follow-up, even if it's three months down the line.

If something really matters to you, it's worth fighting your corner and not giving up. If your boss feels they may never be able to give you whatever it is you need, it may be time to start looking outside of your current company.

You won't know until you ask.

Starting up your own business

Perhaps your career dreams have nothing to do with finding a new job or building on the one you have. Maybe you'd love to go it alone by going self-employed.

If we look at the statistics[15], more women are working now than since comparable records began. There are now 15.6 million of us in the workforce in one capacity or another in the UK alone.

Self-employment is a HUGE area of growth with more than five million women in the UK now running their own businesses. In fact, since 2008 there's been a 69% increase in the number of highly skilled female freelancers (from 528,000 approx. to 893,000).

Women choose to work for themselves because it offers the kind of freedom, flexibility and control that is rarely possible when you're employed by somebody else. This is especially significant for working mothers who want and need to earn a living while spending time with their family. In fact, one in eight of all solo self-employed people are working mothers.

Of course, it's not just mums who make up the ranks of the female self-employed. Young women just starting out in their careers are also choosing to forge their own pathways. Women in their 30s, 40s and beyond are choosing to smash through the glass ceilings of their working lives by building their own businesses on their own terms.

There is a huge amount of advice and support available to help you set up your own business.

I set up Jo Bevilacqua – formerly The Unique Mumpreneur – to help women either set up or grow their businesses with a supportive community cheering them on. We have thousands of women in our Facebook group, She Leads, where all women, not just mothers now, support each other every single day. Feel free to join us, I really would love to see you there.

As part of our community, you will find information and tools about setting up, self-assessment and paying taxes, company types, what to charge, marketing, invoicing, delivering your products or services, customer service, social media and much, much more.

I don't want to cover the ins and outs of starting a business in this chapter because it's a topic that would require a whole book in itself, but I have got a course that you could check out if that was the route you wanted to go down (find out more at jobevilacqua.com).

Instead, as this chapter is about getting what you want from your career, I want to talk about some confidence boosters that may help you to get your own business off the ground.

Adopt the right mindset

The truth is that you may not feel confident about starting a business straight away. This is uncharted territory, so you're likely to feel more than a bit terrified (trust me, I've been there!).

Or maybe you do feel confident and want to hit the ground running.

Either way, here are some thoughts and beliefs that can help you get started and remind yourself why this decision is the right one for you:

* I can and must start this business

* It is what I want for my working life

* I have every ability to figure out how to make this business successful

* What I don't know, I can learn

* When failure hits or I make a mistake, I will learn from it, grow from it and leverage it to create success

* I have a community that I am meant to serve – and they won't be fully served unless I step out of my comfort zone and build this business

* This business is the key to my/my family's financial future – it is my obligation to create financial freedom and long-lasting security for the people I love (and that includes me)

One of the reasons that it's helpful to build a business with these thoughts in your mind is that it shifts the focus away from you – especially what you don't know yet - to who your business can serve. Although this might sound like you're putting yourself last on the list again, you're honestly not.

By focusing on your community, you can set yourself free to create a business that transforms your life while transforming the lives of others.

Think about these questions:

* What does my community need?

* Where is my community struggling?

* How can I help to improve their lives today?

* What knowledge, experience or information can I share with them?

* What else can I do to support and serve my community?

None of these questions are about your insecurities or debating whether you are cut out to run your own business. Instead, they put your customers at the heart of your decision-making. There are people out there who have been waiting for what you can offer for years, maybe decades. They NEED you.

You don't have to be perfect; you just have to show up.

And, if you do it from a place of authenticity within yourself, your tribe will recognise that. If you're able to say running this business means everything to me, it's what my dreams revolve around, your honesty will resonate with your customers.

I love this saying:

"Confidence is not a prerequisite to starting your business; courage is."

Over to you

So, what is it that you want from your future career?

Remember, there is no right or wrong, only what's right for you right now. Your ambitions can change and so can your direction.

Whether self-employed, employed by someone else, part-time, full-time, a working mum, a stay at home mum, volunteering or retraining, YOU CAN DO THIS.

I believe in you.

I see your potential.

Now, start believing in yourself.

Follow your heart and find your tribe. Your tribe are people with similar passions.

- Kanye West

REFLECTION TIME

How do you feel?

_____

_____

_____

What have you learnt?

_____

_____

_____

What will you change?

_____

_____

_____

What will you do more of?

_____

_____

_____

What will you do less of?

_____

_____

_____

Does this raise any strong feelings for you?
(This is your gut telling you that there's a potential issue you need to address)

_____

_____

_____

Do you have any questions?

_____

_____

_____

Chapter 15:

Quality over quantity time

(Why your life doesn't have to go on hold to be a great parent)

We may have established that you've been delaying your dreams and goals because you've been putting everyone and everything before you. I hope that by now you're starting to believe in yourself more than you have done before.

I also hope that you now know you have the potential to achieve whatever you put your mind to and that you can start putting yourself at the top of your own priority list.

But I can imagine that, even if that is the case, there will still be a part of you that feels some sort of guilt for wanting to want different things, change the dynamics, rock the boat, especially when it comes to the effects we tell ourselves it may have on our children.

As I've said earlier in this book, we've somehow been programmed to believe that we have to be with and entertain our kids 24/7 and if we don't, we'll damage them or lack as a mother. Hopefully, this chapter will reassure you this isn't the case and you have the permission to do what is right for you. If that means not being with your children every minute of every day, then so be it.

In recent decades there seems to have been a shift in family dynamics. I read an article back in 2016 by a family psychologist, John Rosemond, who said that if you ask most people who have become parents since the millennium who the most important people are in their family, they will unanimously say 'the kids'[16].

Parents make huge sacrifices to indulge their children's every need and whim, often at significant cost to their own relationships and well-being.

Rosemond, and many other psychologists like him, feel this elevated status can be damaging for children and their parents. He argues that parents have the most important needs because they provide the food, shelter, education, clothing, emotional support, security and all the things that are important for children.

It's Rosemond's belief that parents need to prepare their children to be responsible citizens in adulthood and model the skills to thrive. But, when children believe they are more important than their parents, they risk becoming entitled and feeling that there is nothing they can be taught.

The article resonated so strongly with me because Rosemond urged us, as parents, to redress the balance, stressing how unfair it is for all concerned to put children on a pedestal and ourselves on hold.

Therefore, this chapter is for those of you who are putting yourself last on the list all the time because you feel that you should be ever-present for your kids.

I imagine I will mainly be talking to women here, but if you are a man for whom this resonates then I hope you'll overlook my sweeping generalisations!

In my experience, men rarely feel – or are rarely made to feel – that they have to put themselves on hold to be a good parent. But, as we've seen in other chapters, society tends to have different expectations of women.

And I say, expectations be damned!

Trust me, you can be an outstanding parent and still make time for your own needs.

I believe with all of my heart that only good can come from children having parents who model self-care and individual fulfilment. After all, don't we want our children to be able to live a life that brings them joy and fulfils them personally and professionally? And how better to learn how to achieve that than seeing their parents – in this case, their mum – setting out a road map for living with intention and integrity?

Finding balance

I know that you want to spend time with your kids; no-one is suggesting that you shouldn't. I also get that you may want to be present for all the big stuff in their lives and create a home in which your children feel loved and secure. It's only natural to want those things. Your children deserve them and so do you.

Wanting those things is what drove me to build three successful businesses.

What I'm saying is that you don't have to sacrifice your own needs to accomplish this. It is entirely possible to be there for your kids and to be there for yourself too. It's not always easy. Sometimes it requires compromise. Sometimes it takes time. But it can be your reality.

Personally, I believe that flexibility is the key to a healthy, well-rounded family. It's totally possible to spend time pursuing your own dreams at the same time as nurturing your kids.

All the research suggests that children do best in life when they have quality time with their parents. But quality time doesn't mean all of your time. I think sometimes we confuse quality with quantity, seeing the two as interchangeable when, really, they're not. Your kids won't fall apart if you don't spend every minute of the day with them. In fact, they may grow in exciting and wonderful ways when they're given the space and support to do so.

Quality time has far more long-lasting benefits than an endless quantity of time. Recent neuroscience research has discovered that being with a child is not the most important aspect of their development[17].

What really matters is whether the child is hugged, listened to, shown delight and provided with lots of warm, loving interactions without having to demand them. These are the things that matter far more than a tally of hours in each other's presence.

The question for us as parents should be, 'What does my child need to preserve an emotional connection with me?'

There are families out there who spend every waking moment of the day together and yet never really connect in a meaningful way. I bet most kids would happily trade co-existing without connection for quality time with parents who may have their own interests but who, when they're present, are really present in every way that matters.

Carve out moments of quality time

Something that's worked for my family is building pockets of quality time into our week. For example, when the kids were little we had 'Mummy Mondays' where there was no work, no nursery, no playdates, just us. They had my undivided attention for a whole day. I have tried to keep it going as best I could since they've gone to school, although it's not always possible.

We also try to do a family film night at least once a week where we all take it in turns to choose a film, usually a comedy. There is nothing more in the world that makes me happier than hearing my girls belly laughing. No matter what is going on with work or life, that sound grounds me more than anything else.

My girls often help me with preparing for the networking events I run. They take great pride in being my assistants and spending time with me – plus, they get to learn new skills. And when they come to me with entrepreneurial ideas (which they often do), I'm there to listen and help them work out the details.

The latest thing, which they are working on as I write this, is my eldest being paid to make birthday cakes for friends and family members. Although the cakes are delicious, my kitchen definitely takes a battering.

We try to eat around the table as a family as much as possible throughout the week and it's during our mealtimes that we all chat about our days and things that are happening in our lives. Honestly, this hasn't always been the case. We made a point of doing it when they were toddlers but because the last year things have been somewhat crazy, we found we were doing it less and less. Bedtimes became a bit of a nightmare due to the girls wanting to talk about their whole day when they should be sleeping, and it took me a while to realise it was because we weren't talking about it at dinner. It's safe to say that dinner at the table has been reintroduced and I've got my evenings back, yippee.

Throughout the year, my husband and I make sure that we plan special occasions like day trips with the girls or family holidays. These occasions are a source of mostly happy shared memories, and it gives us all something to look forward to, especially when one or both of us has something big going on with work.

It's by carving out this quality time that we strengthen our bonds as a family. And, thanks to these moments, I think we all feel OK about the times when we focus on the things we each want individually. Whatever we do we all know that we have a special little cheer squad at home, willing us to succeed.

It's feelings that matter

When I think back to my own childhood, I struggle to remember every minute of everyday life. I don't remember every moment my mum and dad spent with me, such as individual bedtimes or post-school afternoons.

What I remember more are the special occasions and the feelings attached with them. The excitement attached to the rare days out to the seaside or to the cinema, the fun we had (and arguments we always got over) playing board games, the reassurance and comfort I got when I had nightmares and was scared.

But most of all I remember always knowing that I was loved. It's the feelings from my childhood that I've carried over into adult life, not a tally of hours my parents were present. And that's what I want my children to take with them into adulthood too.

But what about?

'Whataboutery' and 'comparisonitis', as I like to call them, are two conditions that plague us as parents in modern Western society.

For all of its benefits, social media can be a curse, thanks to the constant deluge of images of picture-perfect mums with their picture-perfect children doing Pinterest-perfect activities from dawn 'til dusk.

It can make you feel like you have to be ever-present, constantly scheduling playdates, extra-curricular activities, crafting opportunities, home baking and so on until the end of time in order to cut it as a parent.

No wonder you feel like your kids might miss out if you're not constantly by their side, doing something for them or with them.

But I want you to really digest what I say now.

IT'S ALL AN ILLUSION!

What parents don't tell you is that the idyllic Instagram shot that sent your guilt into a tailspin took multiple takes, tantrums and bribes before everyone was looking at the camera. Just off-screen to the right of that fun craft activity is a pile of laundry that made it from the washing line to the dining table and is waiting to be folded. That unruffled, ever-smiling mum can't remember the last time she posted an unfiltered photo of herself because she's just so damn tired that the bags under her eyes have turned to suitcases.

Social media only shows us what others want us to see. We don't know what goes on behind closed doors.

Yes, there are some people who take complete fulfilment from being with their kids 24/7 and manage to organise life with the precision of a synchronised swimming team. And that's wonderful if you're one of those people.

All I'm saying is that if you're not, it's totally fine to balance quality family time with time spent on your own growth and development. You don't have to put off prioritising your own needs until some magical day in the future when the kids have flown the nest.

Life is for living TODAY, RIGHT NOW!

REFLECTION TIME

How do you feel?

_____

_____

_____

What have you learnt?

_____

_____

_____

What will you change?

_____

_____

_____

What will you do more of?

_____

_____

_____

What will you do less of?

_____

_____

_____

Does this raise any strong feelings for you?
(This is your gut telling you that there's a potential issue you need to address)

_____

_____

_____

Do you have any questions?

_____

_____

_____

Chapter 16:

Being a good role model

(Why prioritising your own needs is good for your kids)

Our children look to the world around them for their role models. Anyone from a family member or teacher to a world-famous celebrity or favourite YouTuber can influence how they see the world. Some role models are good, some not so good.

We touched on this quite a bit in Chapter 15, but I really want you to think about what it means to be a good role model and how you can exemplify that in your life. This could look different for everyone but I think there is some common ground across all examples.

A good role model is someone who serves as a positive example, inspiring others to live meaningful lives.

Good role models:

* Show passion for the things they love and inspire others to take action

* Have a clear set of values and live in a way that reflects those values

* Are committed to their wider communities and focused on giving in life as well as receiving

* Show selflessness and acceptance of others

* Are resilient and have the ability to overcome obstacles

If we think about being a good role model within the context of parenting, how can you expect your children to reach for the stars if you don't?

Children become what they see

I recently read that the average person says between 300 to 1,000 words to themselves every single minute.[18] Those words can either be positive or they can be a barrage of self-doubt and criticism.[19] It's probably no surprise that what we say to ourselves will depend entirely on the key messages we've been fed all of our lives, particularly in childhood. This is why our children need positive role models.

They need people who will speak to them with kindness and compassion and who will model the skills needed to live a fulfilling, enriching life.

As a parent, you will probably be the first and possibly most enduring role model your child has in their life. You have a choice. You can set examples of resilience and perseverance or you can teach your child to put their needs below everyone else's.

Which do you want for them?

When you take care of yourself

I passionately believe that your children deserve to see you take care of yourself. There's a saying, isn't there, about putting your own oxygen mask on before you attempt to put on anyone else's mask? That absolutely applies to parenting.

You need to take care of yourself before you can give your all to anyone else.

It's also important to recognise that even if you say the most positive, encouraging things to your kids, they will still notice and absorb negative messages if you're uncaring to yourself. Honestly, if your kids hear you being unkind to yourself or see you always putting yourself last, they will learn from this.

I'm not saying this to make you feel stressed or guilty. Parenting is tough enough without me piling the guilt on you. I'm saying this because I want you to show yourself compassion. I want you to stop putting yourself last on the list, not least because your kids deserve a great role model in their lives.

Sometimes you have to break the pattern

Because children become what they see, you may be following patterns of behaviour in your own life that were modelled by your parents. Not all of those patterns may be good.

From today onwards, I'm challenging you to break those patterns once and for all. Continue doing the good stuff that serves you positively and commit to ditching any of the negative habits and associations.

You can decide how to best be a role model to your children, even if it means doing the exact opposite of what you grew up with.

So, what is it that you want for your children?

What skills and values do you want them to learn?

What strengths and characteristics do you think will help them thrive in life?

Now, tell me, why would you not want those same things for yourself?

Because this is what I've noticed in life. As parents, we want the world for our children. We want them to be happy and fulfilled. We want them to do what lights them up inside and to spend time with people who see how amazing they are.

If only we could treat ourselves with the same kindness and care.

Tips for effective role-modelling

When I was planning out this chapter, I did some reading around effective role-modelling and things we can all do to help our kids – and ourselves – feel inspired and empowered. Here are some of my favourite tips:

1.   Include your children in family discussions as it's a great way for

them to see how people communicate and work together

2.   Practice what you preach because children can sniff out hypocrisy a mile-off and they really don't respect it

3.   Work towards a healthy lifestyle by eating well and exercising regularly as it will give your children a blueprint for their own physical wellbeing

4.   Avoid making negative comments about yourself or other people as it will help your children to learn acceptance

5.   Show that you enjoy learning new things

6.   Try to look on the bright side of life, talking and acting in an optimistic way

7.   Take responsibility for your mistakes and talk openly about how you can correct them without seeking to place the blame on other people or circumstances

8.   Let your children see you figuring out the solutions to problems and trying different things as it will give them the confidence to problem solve

9.   Show kindness and respect to others in your words and actions and say sorry when you need to

10.   Model stating your needs or asserting your boundaries so that your children will learn that it's OK to say no or to ask for what they need in life

The last point is important. It's even good practice to set boundaries within your own family. For example, you might say to your children (depending on their age, of course), 'I'm going to spend the next two hours studying/working/creating/reading and I don't want to be disturbed. I would like you to find something to do that you enjoy. Afterwards, we can play a game together/go for a walk/chat.'

If you take just one thing away from reading this book, I hope it's the realisation that putting yourself high on your list of priorities is actually a gift to the people who love you too. It makes you a good role model. It keeps you energised and recharged so you're better able to give to others. It's the difference between surviving and thriving.

Your legacy isn't one thing. Your legacy is every life you've touched.

- Maya Angelou

REFLECTION TIME

How do you feel?

_____

_____

_____

What have you learnt?

_____

_____

_____

What will you change?

_____

_____

_____

What will you do more of?

_____

_____

_____

What will you do less of?

_____

_____

_____

Does this raise any strong feelings for you?
(This is your gut telling you that there's a potential issue you need to address)

_____

_____

_____

Do you have any questions?

_____

_____

_____

Chapter 17:

Setting goals and reaching them

(Bringing to life the vision you want for yourself)

Get your pen and paper ready as you'll need it for this chapter!

We're going to talk about goal setting.

Goal setting is one of those things that some people do religiously, and other people don't even consider.

Some people set goals at least once a year and believe it helps them accomplish their ambitions. Others do it once and then forget about it. Some people focus on what their life will look like in ten years while others can't seem to look past tomorrow.

Whichever category you fit in I want you to give consistent goal setting a try. I think you may be amazed by the results.

What do YOU want?

Goal setting is all about YOUR personal goals and dreams.

What do you want to experience in life? Do you want to own your own home, learn to paint, get fit, travel more, volunteer for a cause you believe in, retire at 50? This isn't about anyone else but you.

As we've seen throughout this book, it can be really hard to think about what you actually want out of life, especially if you've never thought about it before. It can be difficult to think too far ahead or your own doubts might stop you. But it's important to write everything down, no matter how out of reach it may seem to you right now. Include that rescue dog, holiday home or new skill that would give you purpose.

What do you truly want out of life in one, three, five or ten years' time?

There are so many tools and approaches that can help you with setting goals and actually achieving them. These methods can keep you accountable and can motivate you to keep going.

Here's what helps me:

* *Join a mastermind group*

A mastermind group is probably one of my favourite ways to set goals, be kept accountable and then achieve them or acknowledge why you haven't achieved them. Not only do I run mastermind groups, I am also a part of a group that my mentor runs too.

It's basically where a group of six to eight people come together to meet face-to-face on a regular basis to develop their business and personal skills. Every Mastermind member has a chance to talk about the issues they're currently facing and to come up with solutions with the help of the group. As everyone has different experiences, the members can learn from each other, gaining confidence and broadening their perspective with each meeting.

All mastermind groups are different so I can only give you the feedback from my own mastermind. My group starts as a six-month programme so on the very first session we will sit down with all members to go through what their six-month goals are and what they want to achieve by the end of the programme. During each of the subsequent sessions, each member is given actions to complete by the following month, which will help them reach their six-month goals. The individuals then decide on whether they want to continue on their journey together and if so, it turns into a rolling programme.

Masterminds are not the cheapest form of development to join but they are so worth it – the investment definitely pays off!

* *Create a vision board*

Hopefully, you got to grips with creating a vision board back in Chapter 7; if not, now's the time to revisit that chapter.

* *Get an accountability partner*

I think most of us find it easier to stick to goals if we have to be accountable. This is why I often choose to work with an accountability partner.

An accountability partner is someone who's prepared to act as part-cheerleader/part-coach. And, ideally, you will do the same for them. The idea is that you both set targets based on your goals and check-in with one another to make sure you're staying on track.

For example, you might decide to launch an e-course and agree with an accountability partner that you'll have the first module written by the end of the week. The accountability partner has full permission to give you a metaphorical kick up the backside if you start to dither or go off track.

Make sure you choose this person wisely. You don't want them to let you get away with not doing what you need to do to progress or lay into you if life really did get in the way, there's a fine line.

Make your goals SMART

Most experts recommend SMART goals as the secret to setting goals that you will actually follow to completion (you might remember that I mentioned them briefly in Chapter 9).

SMART goals are:

SPECIFIC

MEASURABLE

ACHIEVABLE

REALISTIC/RELEVANT

TIME-BOUND/TIME-SPECIFIC

What does this mean?

Well, people often set goals that are vague and open-ended. For example, 'I want to save enough money to buy a new kitchen'. However, this kind of goal doesn't come with a road map for how you're going to achieve it or when you're going to achieve it.

A SMART goal drills down to the details. It may also relate to a smaller step within the larger goal.

Using our new kitchen example, a SMART goal might say, 'I want to save £5,000 towards a new kitchen within the next 12 months'.

This is measurable because you know how much you want to save and the timeframe you plan to do it in. However, a SMART goal still needs to go a step further. You need to map out how you plan to achieve your goal.

You might make your goal, 'I plan to save £5,000 towards a new kitchen within the next 12 months by launching a four-week e-course that I will sell for £99. To do this, I need to sell the course to 50 people this year. I will need a month to write it before having 11 months to sell it. I will need to sell it to four to five people a month to achieve my goal'.

Can you see how helpful this approach is?

It gives you a really specific way of approaching a goal so that you break it down into manageable chunks.

You can apply this approach to pretty much any personal or professional goal in your life.

Visualising your goals

Many psychologists advise that the best way to actually achieve goals is to visualise the outcome as a reality.

To do this:

* Write down what it is you really want. It's important to aim for clarity here. Describe the outcome in detail – not just what you want to happen but how it will make you feel, how it could change your life, what you could share with your loved ones and even who achieving your goals could make you become.

* The next step is to visualise achieving your goals – let your brain see and experience everything as if your goal has already been reached.

* Talk to yourself positively. Tell yourself that you are capable of reaching your goals. Don't talk about IF you succeed, talk about WHEN.

* Get on with achieving it.

Activity Sixteen: Set your SMART goals

Setting SMART goals can take a bit of practice, so I want you to make a start here. On the next page, I've put together a SMART goal worksheet for you. You can print more off online at:

https://www.jobevilacqua.com/resources/ for subsequent goals.

For now, let's look at one SMART goal that you can work towards

Remember, your SMART goals are a bit like the sections of a route map taking you from A to B to C and so on. Make sure you keep them somewhere that you can refer back to often

SMART GOALS

SPECIFIC	**What do you want to accomplish?**
MEASUREABLE	**How will you know when you have accomplished your goal?**
ATTAINABLE	**What steps do you need to take? What skills and resources will you need?**
REALISTIC	**How will you make it achievable?**
TIMELY	**When is the deadline for your goal?**

Slow success will build your character. Quick success will build your ego.

Choose wisely.

- Unknown

REFLECTION TIME

How do you feel?

_____

_____

_____

What have you learnt?

_____

_____

_____

What will you change?

_____

_____

_____

What will you do more of?

_____

_____

_____

What will you do less of?

_____

_____

_____

Does this raise any strong feelings for you?
(This is your gut telling you that there's a potential issue you need to address)

_____

_____

_____

Do you have any questions?

_____

_____

_____

Chapter 18:

Planning for success

(How to make your time count)

As you've worked through this book, I hope you've started to build a clearer idea about what success would look like for you and, most importantly, what makes you happy.

Now, it's time to take action.

'I haven't got time,' you might say. But, honestly, if you haven't got time for yourself today, when will you have time? What are you waiting for?

Please, please, please stop putting your needs on hold until some mythical time in the future when you can concentrate on yourself.

That day will never come unless you choose it.

The last thing I want is for you to wake up ten years from now full of regret about all the things you didn't do. We don't know what lies ahead, so we have to live for today.

My experience is that, actually, we can make time for anything we set our minds to. It's just a case of deciding what you want to prioritise. I bet if one of your kids needed you to help them achieve something, even if it was a project for school, you would find that time from somewhere. I want you to do the same for yourself. The magic in life happens where we put our focus. But, as I've already said, you have to choose where your focus will be.

Dream big

Throughout this book, I've urged you to conjure up your dreams and imagine what it would feel like to realise them.

I hope you've let yourself dream, the bigger the better. Because why shouldn't you dream? Why shouldn't you aim for the accomplishments and feelings in life that would empower and fulfil you?

Even if you were to fall short of your biggest dream, just imagine what you could achieve while striving towards it.

Managing your time

I want you to begin blocking out some time to work on your dreams. This could be working towards launching your own business, more time for a hobby or self-care, applying for a promotion or study and personal development. The goals are entirely your own.

Personally, I find it really helpful to have a wall planner or printed diary in front of me so that I can physically schedule in time devoted to my SMART goals (remember those from Chapter 17?). You could use an online diary, calendar or planner if you prefer. Again, it's about finding whatever works for you.

At the end of this chapter, I've included copies of my daily, weekly and monthly planners that you can use. You can print off extra copies from: https://www.jobevilacqua.com/resources/

Having your SMART goals in front of you will help you work out the deadlines you set for specific goals and how you need to plan your time from now until then to achieve what you want.

Look at the next 12 months overall for the big picture stuff. However, you'll need to break things down into how you want to spend your time over the next day, week, month and quarter.

What I find works best for me is to put the non-negotiables on my planner first. This covers everything from work commitments to school events I plan to attend or evenings with friends, holidays and days off. These are fixed points in my diary that I can't or don't want to cancel.

My next step is to earmark dedicated blocks of time in my diary to focus on my goals. I might have a few hours in the week dedicated to necessary admin tasks for my businesses but also chunks of time that I spend on strategy.

When writing this book, there were times that I had to book half days or full days out of my diary to get it finished in time. I had a deadline to launch, therefore there were things in the lead up to that date that had to be done, regardless of whatever else was going on at work or at home.

Once these blocks of time are in my diary, I treat them like my non-negotiables. They are appointments that I keep with the same commitment I would show to a client who has booked in time to work with me.

This commitment is absolutely crucial to my success. I know it's so easy to push time like this to one side, especially if something unexpected comes up. So many of us are guilty of doing this, but what message does it give? Every time you cancel the time you planned to spend on meeting your own needs, you send yourself a subconscious message that you're not worth prioritising.

My advice is that once time is blocked off in your planner, you view it as absolute. If you need to find time to deal with an emergency, beg, borrow or steal it from a less important time in your week if at all possible.

Remember to control the controllables

I want you to skip back to Chapter 11 in a moment. This is when we talked about controlling the controllable in your life and letting go of anything that you couldn't influence.

If there are things that you want to change, achieve or even eliminate from your life, you will need to plan time to focus on the next steps. Block the time into your diary.

Remember, where you put your focus is where the magic happens.

DAILY PLANNER FOR SUCCESS!!

Date:

Time	
5am	
6am	
7am	
8am	
9am	
10am	
11am	
midday	
1pm	
2pm	
3pm	
4pm	
5pm	
6pm	
7pm	
8pm	
9pm	
10pm	

CALLS TO MAKE

3 GOOD THINGS

1.

2.

3.

THINGS TO BUY

TODAYS MENU

Breakfast	
Snack	
Lunch	
Snack	
Dinner	

EMAILS TO SEND

JUST FOR ME

DOODLES

WATER INTAKE

DAILY CHORES

SOCIAL MEDIA UPDATE

NOTES

DAILY EXERCISE

Aim	minutes
Done	minutes

"To be organised
is to be in control"

$\mathrm{J_B}$ | WEEKLY PLAN   Week:

THIS WEEKS MAIN FOCUS

WHAT WILL I DO MORE OF

WHAT WILL I DO LESS OF

PERSONAL TASKS

PERSONAL GOALS

THINGS I WILL ACHIEVE

THINGS I AM GRATEFUL FOR THIS WEEK

THINGS I HAVE LEARNT THIS WEEK

$\mathrm{J_B}$ | JO BEVILACQUA

$\mathbf{J_B}$ | MONTHLY PLAN   Month:

THIS MONTHS MAIN FOCUS

WHAT WILL I DO MORE OF

WHAT WILL I DO LESS OF

PERSONAL TASKS

PERSONAL GOALS

THINGS I WILL ACHIEVE

THINGS I AM GRATEFUL FOR THIS MONTH

THINGS I HAVE LEARNT THIS MONTH

$\mathbf{J_B}$ | JO
BEVILACQUA

REFLECTION TIME

How do you feel?

_____

_____

_____

What have you learnt?

_____

_____

_____

What will you change?

_____

_____

_____

What will you do more of?

_____

_____

_____

What will you do less of?

_____

_____

_____

Does this raise any strong feelings for you?
(This is your gut telling you that there's a potential issue you need to address)

_____

_____

_____

Do you have any questions?

_____

_____

_____

I'm no longer available for things that make me feel like shit.

- Unknown

Chapter 19:

Self-care

(Why I hope you're no longer last on the list)

Here we are – the final chapter. I hope beyond all hope that you feel very differently today to how you felt when you opened this book for the first time. I hope you now see how important it is that you stop putting yourself last in your own life?

I hope I've shown you that when you prioritise yourself, it actually acts as a positive for everyone around you. Someone who takes care of their own needs is better able to support others, be a good role model, exude positivity and contribute to their wider community. It's a win-win.

From today onwards, I want you to commit to investing in yourself, your mindset and your learning.

I want to hear that you're planning quality 'me' time and celebrating it instead of feeling guilty.

I want to know that you're owning your dreams and focused on making them happen.

In case I haven't convinced you yet, I'm going to say it again.

YOU ARE IMPORTANT.

You are as entitled to take up space in this world as anyone else. You deserve to live a life that is fulfilling and authentic and aligned to your values. You shouldn't have to wait for some distant day in the far-off future to put your own needs high up on your list of priorities.

You are not promised tomorrow, next week or next year. The only thing we really have is today, this moment here, and it's down to you what you choose to do with it.

Being self-full is not selfish, so do whatever it takes to be self-full.

Top of the list

Once you begin caring for yourself, it will hopefully become a life-long habit. You will get better at it with practice, so don't beat yourself up if you find it tough at first.

You will always be a work in progress. We all are. Personally, I think it's a good thing.

The nature of life is that it's ever moving and often runs in circles or unexpected directions. People change. Dreams change. And you will need to keep revisiting what you want from life.

I love this though. I love knowing that I'm a different person today to the person I was ten years ago. And I'll be different again ten years from now. I'm excited to see who I'll become. I hope you feel the same way about yourself and all the wonderful parts of you waiting to be discovered.

Life is about constantly learning, growing and evolving. If it wasn't, we would just be standing still and how boring would that be?!

I hope this book has been a helpful tool on this part of your journey and that you'll use it time and time again, working through it regularly as you grow and your goals change. As much as I have loved sharing this part of your journey with you, this is your life, you have your vision and now I'm going to hand the reins over to you.

You might be a mum, daughter, sister, wife, partner, niece, grandmother, aunt, carer, friend, boss, team member – or wear a multitude of other hats – but, above all, you are uniquely you.

And you, my love, deserve to come first on your list.

Revisit the activities (often)

Have you found the activities throughout the book helpful? You may be wondering what to do with them next. My advice is to buy yourself a special folder, the glitzier and brighter the better (or is that just me and my hopeless stationery addiction?)

Put all of the activities in the file and revisit them often. In fact, put a note in your diary now to revisit the activities at least once a month. I want you to keep visualising your dreams or challenging those limiting beliefs. Remember what I said at the beginning of the book? This isn't a one-time-only thing.

As you start to see positive change in your life, reuse the activities that resonate most powerfully. For example, I always update my vision board and SMART goals because they keep me on track. Stick affirmations or pictures above your desk or carry them in your handbag. Talk to your friends about your goals.

Dare to dream and to take up all the space you need in this world. Don't ever feel guilty for stating your needs.

The world needs you, as your true, fulfilled, happy self.

Final thoughts

I decided to finally write this book just as parts of the world were going into lockdown due to the COVID-19 pandemic in 2020. Schools began to close, jobs were furloughed and women made up the majority of 'frontline' workers. I realised that women would probably be disproportionately affected by what was about to unfold.

It seemed more important to me than ever to give women a voice and put a fire in their bellies to claim a seat at the table in the world post-COVID and, if that didn't work, to set up their own damn table.

The stats speak for themselves. According to Catalyst – a group supporting the rights of women in the workforce – 60% of essential workers during the pandemic were women[20]. Specifically, though, women were in 77% of the jobs considered 'high risk' for contracting COVID-19. At the same time, women were 5% more likely to have lost their job due to the pandemic.

The Guardian described the UK's working mothers as 'sacrificial lambs' as 50% of us were unable to access the childcare we needed to return to work[21]. A staggering 67% of working mums had to reduce their hours due to a lack of childcare, while 30.5% of pregnant key workers were suspended from work on incorrect terms, such as being forced to take sick leave or start their maternity leave early.

Of the 15% of women overall who were made redundant due to COVID-19, lack of childcare factored into 46% of those cases. At the same time, 74% of self-employed women saw a significant drop in their earning capacity because of having no access to childcare.

The figures are staggering but this book isn't just about that one period in time. All these statistics do is provide a snapshot of the challenges we face every day as women.

Inequalities such as lower pay, lower status and fewer opportunities at work are just the tip of the iceberg. Women are also disproportionately affected by a lack of affordable childcare and we shoulder more than our fair share of housework. As this book attests, many of us are exhausted by the so-called 'hidden burden' of family life. Appointments, haircuts, holiday planning, Christmas, birthdays, anniversaries, school events, inset days, deadlines, pets, washing, cleaning – we're holding all of those things in our heads and more.

This book is about finding a way to share the load and spearhead positive change.

I believe with all my heart that women are strongest when we work together and lift each other up. The only way to tackle the gender inequalities in our society is to shine a light on them before pushing back and demanding more. The more of us who speak up, the harder it will be for society to ignore our voices. I feel positive about the path ahead and look forward to witnessing more glorious women claiming their dreams.

I truly hope that you have enjoyed reading this book as much as I have enjoyed writing it. Each chapter has served as an important reminder that we only get one shot at this beautiful, messy, complicated thing called life. Instead of making me sad, it's a realisation that puts fire in my belly. I hope you feel the same.

Acknowledgements

As the African proverb states, 'If you want to go fast go alone, if you want to go far go together'.

Writing a book is much the same as any other journey that you go on and one that I could never have done justice to alone.

I feel I've been truly blessed to have met the people and experienced the things that I have. Now I'm not saying all of them have been positive experiences, far from it, BUT I am saying that each and every person and situation has taught me something, and I wouldn't be the person I am today without all of them.

As a people lover, there are just too many to thank, but I'll attempt a few and hope I don't offend anyone I've accidentally missed.

My mum and dad, without your bravery, independence and want for a better life, I literally wouldn't be here today. You are like chalk and cheese but fate brought you together all those years ago and I'm so glad it did. You both support me in your own, amazing ways. I truly believe I am half of both of you, and I have clearly inherited all the best personality traits from each of you: kindness, trustworthiness, straight-talking, generosity, honesty, loyalty and being fun, haha. On a serious note, I thank you for teaching me from a young age and instilling in me all the core values I live by everyday. I promise to teach the girls the same lessons.

My little sis Sabrina, my first best friend, my first pride and joy and my number one protector! I am so proud of you and the journey you are on. You are and have always been so much stronger, wiser and more beautiful than you give yourself credit for. I cannot wait to continue watching you flourish and be happier than you ever thought possible and watch the boys grow into great young men that you helped them become.

My girlfriends, there's so many of you with whom I've shared laughter, tears and lessons over the years but special shoutouts to the ladies that have been there consistently: Becky, Nicola, Melissa, Laura, Andrea, Amy and Anna. We may not speak everyday or every month even but when we get together, it's like we've never been apart.

My best friend Nicki, there is nothing I could ever write that could fully explain what you and our friendship means to me. From 13 years old you have been my constant, the yin to my yang, the salt to my pepper. Your unwavering support and friendship is something I would never want to live without. Many people associate soulmates with a romantic relationship but in this case I disagree, you really are my soulmate and I'm the luckiest person in the world because of it. We have been through it all together and I hope to always be there for you as you continue to smash the ceilings of your goals, be there for your children as they grow too and laugh all the way into an old people's home, together.

My bestie Natalie, our friendship has truly lasted the test of time. We have been through it all together, from partying every night and girlie holidays to getting married and having kids together. You have always been so caring and supportive and have made me laugh more than anyone in the world! One day we will write a book of all the crazy stuff we've been through, although I'm not sure anyone else will find it as funny as we do! Thank you for always being there, always listening to my rants and reasons and for always making me belly laugh more than anyone else in the world.

My husband Adam, when they say everything happens for a reason, it has never been truer than with us. I was in awe of your handsomeness from the first moment I saw you, at 17 years old in The College Arms (classy) and although we both knew there was something between us then, I'm so glad we didn't pursue it. I think it is fair to say it would NEVER have worked. Fast forward some six years later and bumping into you on what was a last minute night out for both of us changed the course of our lives forever. From a bit of fun to shacking up and getting pregnant within months, you were and still are exactly what I wanted and needed – chilled out, laid back, the silent supporter, the person who always allows me to be fully me, unconditionally. You have given me the two greatest gifts I could ever have asked for and although I know I give you a hard time at times, I could never have done what I have done and achieved what I have without you. Like a version of Sliding Doors, meeting you single-handedly changed my life forever.

Linda and Peter, I understand that I probably came into your family like a wrecking ball but I just want to say how grateful I am for both of you. You welcomed me in from day one and have always gone out of your way to help Adam and I, especially with the girls. You are great people, great parents and even better grandparents. Thank you for all that you do and all that you are. Our lives are richer because of you.

To my right hand women Emma and Chelsie, I am so glad that you both came into my world. You have both been there from the beginning of each business you support me in and I couldn't imagine you not being by my side as the businesses continue to grow. The two of you are so patient with me when I come up with all these new ideas that I want to implement yesterday and always give it your all. You have both grown so much from your first days with me and I'm so glad I could be there to witness it all. Thank you for everything you do for me and the businesses.

To the rest of my teams, thank you for all that you do, I hope you enjoy being a part of my vision as much as I love having you there, the businesses wouldn't be what they are without you. A special thank you to Natalie too – the way you have stepped up this last year has been incredible and I am so proud of you, thank you.

James B, my brother from another mother. You were the first person to positively communicate the potential you saw in me, the person who openly saw my potential way before I saw it in myself. I don't think you could ever appreciate or understand the impact you had on me at such a critical time in my life. A flippant question in conversation turned into my favourite job ever, a team that I loved being a part of, a summer I will never forget and a found obsession for sales and helping people. The lessons and skills learnt in that time of my life have made me the business person and woman I am today and a big part of that is down to you. Thank you for being the big brother I needed.

To all the women in my community, thank you for trusting me to help you in your journey, thank you for being the women that lift each other up rather than tear each other down. Thank you for showing up and supporting each other without judgement. I adore each and everyone of you and I'm excited to see where we all go from here. I feel like this so just the beginning of something wonderful and I'm excited to be by your side every step of the way.

Special kudos to my business babes turned business besties. Business is always personal and I'm so glad that I have you all (The Vault & The Cartel) – our relationships have developed into friendship and I know you have my back as much as I have yours.

To Hannah, Ella, Tracey, and Morgan, you believed in my vision when that's all it was and you continue to support whenever you can, thank you for not only being a business support but a personal support too.

Thank you to Emma H and Rosie who helped me bring this book to life. I know it might not have been the easiest book to work on or me the easiest author (eek) but I hope it was all worth it. Thank you so much for being so patient and encouraging, I couldn't have done it without you both.

To Shaa, picking up your book in an airport whilst on a hen do in Amsterdam opened a whole new world of opportunity to me. I went from coasting and complacency to finding my purpose and enthusiasm. You encourage me to embrace myself fully and live my life as authentically me. When I have a wobble about being misunderstood or 'too much', you are always there to remind me that those who mind don't matter and those who matter don't mind; it's about attracting those that accept us and repelling the ones who don't. That is a life lesson in itself. I am so glad that I attracted you into my life and that I have you in my corner, I will always be so grateful for your support and your kick up the ass (just not the running or the half marathons, I will NEVER be grateful for that). Thank you for always pushing me and seeing me when I struggle to see myself.

Michelle, I truly feel like I hit the jackpot when you came into my life. From a random Fb ad promoting the Small Awards to meeting you, falling in love with you and your campaign; supporting small businesses in the UK, to now being able to call you a friend and one of my biggest cheerleaders. I honestly feel like the luckiest person in the world, I am so much stronger having you support me and pushing me out of my comfort zone and I hope one day I can pay you back somehow. I am in absolute awe of everything you are and everything you do; you are a real life superwoman and everyone's life is richer because of you.

To my greatest achievement and my biggest blessing, my girls. I found this the hardest part of the whole book to write. While I have so much I want to say to you and about you, I'm also conscious that what I put into writing is forever, and I don't want my own thoughts or opinions to influence you consciously or unconsciously in any way shape or form.

What I will say is that I am so deeply honoured to be your mummy, you both make me want to do better and be better.

You are both so special in your own right and I know that not only have you changed my life but you will continue to grow and change the lives of others. You are both so kind, so caring and so determined, and although that is challenging at times, I love that you know the power of your voice and you are not afraid to use it.

I hope I have been a good mummy, a mummy that you're proud of and one who has helped you really believe that you are capable of anything. As you age I hope you look back on your memories growing up with fondness but are equally equipped to move forward with strength and an unbreakable inner confidence.

Above all, I hope you always value your worth, have strong boundaries, and always, always, put yourself first on the list.

I love you always and forever my babies, stay forever happy xx

References

1. Chapter 3, https://time.com/3640988/jennifer-aniston-woman-kids-fulfill-you/

2. Chapter 3, https://hbswk.hbs.edu/item/kids-of-working-moms-grow-into-happy-adults

3. Chapter 3, https://www.ncbi.nlm.nih.gov/pmc/articles/PMC4860719/

4. Chapter 3, https://journalistsresource.org/studies/economics/jobs/working-mother-employment-research/

5. Chapter 3, https://www.gsb.stanford.edu/insights/eric-bettinger-why-stay-home-parents-are-good-older-children

6. Chapter 3, https://ghk.h-cdn.co/assets/cm/15/12/55071e0298a05_-_Involving-children-in-household-tasks-U-of-M.pdf

7. Chapter 3, https://news.vistaprint.com/wp-content/uploads/2016/09/Vistaprint-Woman-Owned-Micro-Business-report.pdf

8. Chapter 6, https://smallbusiness.co.uk/mothers-take-pay-cut-2538646/

9. Chapter 12, https://medium.com/the-polymath-project/you-are-the-average-of-the-five-people-you-spend-the-most-time-with-a2ea32d08c72

10. Chapter 12, https://www.verywellmind.com/top-reasons-to-smile-every-day-2223755

11. Chapter 12, https://www.goodandkind.org/stories/blog/the-power-of-smiling

12. Chapter 12, https://www.happify.com/hd/why-you-should-write-a-gratitude-journal/

13. Chapter 14, https://www.psychologytoday.com/us/blog/thrive/201102/finding-happiness-work

14. Chapter 14, https://business.linkedin.com/content/dam/me/business/en-us/talent-solutions-lodestone/body/pdf/Gender-Insights-Report.pdf

15. Chapter 14, https://www.ipse.co.uk/policy/research/women-in-self-employment/women-in-self-employment-report.html

16. Chapter 15, https://www.stuff.co.nz/life-style/parenting/87930732/why-your-kids-should-not-be-the-most-important-people-in-your-family

17. Chapter 15, https://www.parentspartner.com/quality-time/

18. Chapter 16, https://nathanwood.consulting/2017/11/13/the-power-of-self-talk/

19. Chapter 16, http://www.qungasvik.org/additional//04.pdf

20. Final thoughts, https://www.catalyst.org/research/covid-19-job-loss/

21. Final thoughts, https://www.theguardian.com/money/2020/jul/24/uk-working-mothers-are-sacrifical-lambs-in-coronavirus-childcare-crisis?CMP=share_btn_fb

Before you go...

I really have loved sharing this journey with you and if you're up for it, I would love to get to know you better. If this book has helped you in any way or if you feel I'm missing something, I want to know.

I am someone who not only talks the talk but also walks the walk so, as part of that, I want to know what stood out to you, what helped or resonated with you and what you think is missing. There is always room for growth and not only do I embrace that but I also encourage it.

So, why not drop me an email at bookfeedback@jobevilacqua.com to let me know what you think AND, more importantly, what your plans are moving forward?

I can't wait to hear from you. If you have enjoed the book I would love for you to tell your friends and family about it and shout out about it on your social media profiles. Don't forget to tag me in your posts and use the hashtags #nolongerlast #selffullnotselfish #nolongerlastonthelist

About the author

Jo Bevilacqua is the multi-award-winning founder of Hallmark Carpets and Flooring, Serenity Loves (a beauty salon with on-site crèche) and Jo Bevilacqua Mentoring (formerly The Unique Mumpreneur). She has made such a success of her businesses she has been invited to the House of Lords and Buckingham Palace for the impact her businesses make on her local community. She always puts people over profits which is why she has grown three strong brands that employees love to work for and clients love to be a part of.

Jo is married and a besotted mum to two beautiful girls and a dog called Junior, so she knows a thing or two about juggling many responsibilities.

Day to day, Jo works with business owners to help them grow profitable and productive businesses. She also knows how important it is to work towards a successful life as well as a successful business because business is always personal, especially for small business owners.

Jo openly admits she has been through the many highs and lows building her three businesses from scratch around a young family. She lives and breathes the advice she gives in No Longer Last on the List and encourages you, like the mentor she is, to stop putting your dreams off until tomorrow and start working on them today, because she knows you're truly worth it.

Visit jobevilacqua.com or find Jo's thriving community of busy women just like you at facebook.com/groups/SheLeadsOfficial